From Average to Awesome

Lessons for Living an Extraordinary Life

Jim Smith Jr.

ASTD
PRESS

Alexandria, Virginia

© 2008 the American Society for Training & Development and Jim Smith Jr.

All rights reserved. Printing in the United States of America.

12 11 10   3 4 5 6 7 8

No part of this publication may be reproduced, distributed, or transmitted in any form or by any means, including photocopying, recording, or other electronic or mechanical methods, without the prior written permission of the publisher, except in the case of brief quotations embodied in critical reviews and certain other noncommercial uses permitted by copyright law. For permission requests, please go to www.copyright.com, or write Copyright Clearance Center (CCC), 222 Rosewood Drive, Danvers, MA 01923 (telephone: 978.750.8400, fax: 978.646.8600).

ASTD Press is an internationally renowned source of insightful and practical information on workplace learning and performance topics, including training basics, evaluation and return on investment, instructional systems development, e-learning, leadership, and career development.

Ordering information: Books published by ASTD Press can be purchased by visiting our website at store.astd.org or by calling 800.628.2783 or 703.683.8100.

Poems quoted on pp. 24 and 88 are taken from Janet Cheatham Bell, *Famous Black Quotations and Some Not So Famous* (Chicago: Sabayt Publications, 1986).

Library of Congress Control Number: 2007941492

ISBN-10: 1-56286-534-X
ISBN-13: 978-1-56286-534-4

ASTD Press Editorial Staff:
Director: Cat Russo
Manager, Acquisitions & Author Relations: Mark Morrow
Editorial Manager: Jacqueline Edlund-Braun
Editorial Assistant: Maureen Soyars
Retail Trade Manager: Yelba Quinn

Copyeditor: Alfred F. Imhoff
Indexer: April Davis
Proofreader: Kris Patenaude
Interior Design and Production: PerfecType, Nashville, TN
Cover Design: Ana Ilieva
Cover Illustration: Pete McArthur (room), Slawomir Jastrzebski (sky)

Printed by Victor Graphics Inc., Baltimore, Maryland

This book is dedicated to my mother, R. Nanci Smith. Mom, you gave me life, my spirit, my drive, and my passion for helping others to become awesome. I owe you everything. Thank you for your love, your lessons, and for your never-ending support. I can *always* count on you! I'm so proud to be your son! You are indeed one of a kind!

CONTENTS

FOREWORD

It has been said that experience is the best teacher. I think that's partially true. I believe that we can avoid a lot of pain, failure, and disappointments in life by learning from the positive and negative experiences of others to maximize our own growth and development in life. This book has been written to empower you to transform your life from average to awesome.

As you read and absorb each page, you will discover mind-expanding thoughts and ideas that will inspire you to soar to new heights. Exposure to the key turning points in everyday people's lives will give you knowledge and insights that will enable you to avoid some of the dangerous, treacherous waters of life and get in touch with your own purpose and mission.

Jim will be the first to say that this life-skills book was written in a style and language that everybody could relate to and identify with. The messages and concepts are common sense but not common practice. I believe that most people today are seeking and searching for meaning and significance, more so than ever before. Each chapter of this book will provide you with the necessary keys to unlock the door of your unlimited potential to live a life of contribution, passion, and purpose.

You owe it to yourself to take some quiet time from the noise and distractions of the world and get into this book. I guarantee you, based upon my own experience after reading it, you will never be the same again. It will change your life! Jim, you've done yourself proud!

—**Les Brown**
World-renowned motivational speaker,
best-selling author, radio and television personality,
and Mrs. Mamie Brown's baby boy

ACKNOWLEDGMENTS

I'm blessed to have so many incredible people in my life and in my corner. I refer to them as my Anchors and my Titans. Because of their unfailing strength, support, guidance, patience, love, motivation, leadership, and goal and role modeling, I'm able to thrive, come alive, and, yes, survive. They were the keys to my completing this arduous and inspiring project. They provided counsel and "just in time" hugs and encouragement. They also gave me feedback and space to grow, to write, to fly, and to continue my journey from average to awesome. Thank you so much!

My Anchors: Gina, Mom, Rodney, Daecia, Lauren, Jordan, and Ian.

My Titans: I have numerous Titans in my life. If I listed them all, I would probably have to title this book, *Jim's Titans* rather than *From Average to Awesome*. Let me take this opportunity to especially acknowledge several of them: "Nana" (Mary Lee Faulks), Aunt Venessa, Aunt Cookie, Aunt Lillian, Aunt Gail, Uncle Reggie, Cousin Carol, my sister-in-law Michelle, my nephews Donovan and Joshua, and my other wonderful family members. In addition: Anthony and Carmen Spann, Carolyn Carter, Kathy Cook, Raimond and Bionda Honig, Yolanda Rocio-

Fleming, James and Veronica Gallman, Michael Thompson, Joe Boswell, Nancy Rebecca, Lynn Roman, Catherine Woods, Marilyn Massaro, Aileen Dizon, Leslie Shields, Michael Robinson, Brian and Raenonna Prince, Yvonne Reid-Sissons, Barbara Stern, Patti DeRosa, Mary Ellen Russell, Lisa Nichols, Bill and Lynn Hart, Arvon Jordan, Paul and Danielle Kallmeyer, Sherry Nottingham, John Pace, Kathy Dempsey, Deloris A. Davis, Judy Chapman, Dawn Ridenhour, Annette Stewart, Pauline Shadding, Tony Simmons, Terry Simmons, Roberta Ross, Becky Bottaro, Barry A. Callender, Fayruz Kirtzman and the other members of the Simmons team, Anthony Graham, Bruce Scagel, Kathy Gilbert, Griff and Meena Barger, Barb Kompelein, Sandi Dufault, Keith Baudin, Diane Chew, June Becker, Bobbi Foster, Jane Elliott, Steve and Judy Kane, Sonny and Meryl Elia, Sharon Gerlach, Jeanne Bray, Janae Bower, Loraine Ballard Morrill, Maria Garaitonandia, Trina Crockett, Ceasar and Evelyn Smith, Shelby Moore, Kim Reed, Tonya Murphy, Ron Mitchell, Darin and Cheryl Toliver, Wilma Williams, Della Clark, Pastor Kevin and Kemya Johnson, Jane Moses, Kim Forde, Nancy McGonigle, Kelley Cornish, John Huff, Crystal Reilly, Nancy Appleman-Vassil, Wendy Wolfe, Laura Putnam, Lynette Landing, Shelly Michas, Josh Davies, Suran Casselle, Jim Brown, Renee Russell, Allison Manswell, Mary Ann D'Angelo, and Uneeka Jay. After you read the book, if you would like, you can write your name here _____.

I always have room for more Titans in my life.

I also want to give a huge thank you to my friends, colleagues, clients, and supporters who contributed to the Awesome Advice sidebars and quotations that you'll be reading in the book. Along with my Titans, they are Dr. Frank "Tick" Johnson, Adrianne M. Winter, Priscilla Shumway, Bonnie Strand, Assunta "Susie" F. Marino, Roberta Salisbury, Bettina Carey, Kimberly Reynolds, Doug "Waffleman" McCallum, Hannah G. Gomberg, Jey

Willis, Joe Sparacino, Kim Schreck, Laura Bruner, Elmer Smith, Lisa Dommer, Laura Hughes, Lisa Marzullo, Barbara Rivera, Lorainne Hicks, Rajean Bifano, Paul F. Hafner, Renne Gallart, Shannon Percy, Sheryl B. Craun, Ann Perington, Dan Kropp, Tina M. Greene, Tracie Johnson, and Les Brown.

Introduction:
From Grade School,
to the School of Hard
Knocks, to Awesome!

> Dear James,
> It has been a pleasure to teach you and to know you.
>
> Keep your ideas, your sense of responsibility, your willingness to work, and your pleasing personality—and life should be good to you.
>
> May you have a life of service and happiness!
>
> —MRS. AUDREY BRODIE, JUNE 23, 1979

This book project began nearly seven years ago.

I sat on the floor in a familiar position, my back leaning against the numerous authors on the bookshelf, my legs crossed, ankles overlapped. My subconscious pressed the rewind button in my brain and took me on another fascinating trip down memory lane. With my University City High School

Class of '79 yearbook nestled comfortably in my lap, I turned each page in slow motion, savoring and inhaling every memory, every photo, and every signature.

Some 55 minutes later, I reached the faculty pages and there she was, beaming—my mentor, every lazy senior's nightmare, the lady who was the gatekeeper for umpteen students' diplomas or summer school plans, Mrs. Audrey Brodie.

The chairperson of the school's National Honor Society and my 12th-grade English teacher, Mrs. Brodie was a treasure. With graying hair, pristine grammar, an Estelle (*Golden Girls*) Getty wardrobe and as absolute as a judge demanding quiet in a noisy courtroom, she was a living institution. If educators ever created a Mount Rushmore for teachers, her face would undoubtedly be featured.

Mrs. Brodie conjugated verbs, assigned oral book reports, and jackhammered English theory into students' heads as if this would be their last chance . . . and sadly, in many cases, it was. During her 40-plus years in the classroom, she even taught former basketball legend Wilt Chamberlain.

This superteacher was the reason I majored in English in college. She was the reason my focus in graduate school was journalism. She was the reason I fell in love with Shakespeare, with poetry, with creative writing. She was the reason I knew that one day, some day, eventually, when I finally got around to it, when I stopped putting off the inevitable, I would write the book you're now reading.

While sitting there studying her words, I imagined Mrs. Brodie, propped behind her desk, directly in front of the blackboard saying, "James Smith." ("Yes Mrs. Brodie," I replied.) "It's time to write your book."

Although I didn't know it at the time, Mrs. Brodie had given me a gift that would move *me* from average to awesome—a gift of encouragement, of promise, of hope, of confidence that I would someday succeed in ways I could not even fathom at the time. Perhaps you can think of someone like Mrs. Brodie who took the time to put a life-changing gift right in your lap. Did your own Mrs. Brodie move you, change you, or stop you in your tracks with a single challenging statement? Or was it the strong, proud, unflappable example of a life well lived that moved you and drove you toward change? When you think of that person and the gift of his or her life, are you still moved to tears? If so, then you can understand and appreciate what it could be like to live an awesome life. In the end, that's what this book is all about. *From Average to Awesome* is all about finding, savoring, using, and living with that perfect breath-stopping moment when you finally "get it" and understand the power of living an extraordinary life.

After that special, reflective moment, I was on a semi-mission to write this book. I say "semi" because for the first 12 months or so, my mission consisted solely of my telling people that I was writing a book. That became problem number one. I told my relatives. I told my friends. I told the participants in my management development and creative training workshops. I told the people who came to hear my keynote motivational speeches. I told the people who sat next to me on the plane. I told my listeners who tuned in my radio show each week. I told more people about my writing a book than Bob Barker and Drew Carey's announcer has told to contestants to "Come on down" on *The Price Is Right*.

Everyone knew Jim Smith Jr. was writing a book . . . everyone but my fingers. They waited and waited and waited, patiently, painstakingly, embarrassingly for me to begin.

When I finally decided on the angle, I got recharged. I was going to write a book that was semiautobiographical, focusing on strategies people could incorporate into their lives to be awesome at home, at work, at school, and so on. I did not care that my book would be the 2,222,222,222nd self-help book. My book, I knew, was going to be different. It was going to be a combination of Les Brown and Ellis Cose, mixed with Pat Croce, Oprah Winfrey, Richard Carlson, and Wayne Dyer and seasoned with Iyanla Vansant and Ralph Wiley.

From a motivational and from a personal standpoint, my book was going to really *stretch* the reader. The book was not going to be just your typical "rah rah," hug everyone, eat the right foods, list your top five goals and post them on the refrigerator, promise to have a better attitude for 21 consecutive days, get on the treadmill every day and say "I can do it" motivational book. My approach was going to be more personable, more poignant, more revealing, and as conversational and candid as other books of this genre. Just as important, I was going to "keep it real."

Because I have enjoyed many pats on the back and have endured many kicks in the seat of my personal, academic, and corporate pants, I thought my perspective might be curiously insightful, helpful, and, perhaps, surprising to all my readers. I decided to share many of the hurdles I've had to clear to move from average to awesome. One of those hurdles happens to be race. During my journey to awesomeness, I have grown accustomed to playing the Jackie Robinson role in many of my endeavors. On academic, athletic, and corporate teams, at parties, facilitating workshops, or on business trips, I've learned how to fit in and how to flourish. Elaborating on this hurdle, I thought, would undoubtedly take people on a continuous 15-inch journey—the longest 15 inches in the world—the distance between one's head and one's heart.

I knew some of my readers would wonder why I decided to even mention race. They would wonder why, because I've been relatively successful in life, I have to play the race card. I knew that some of them would not understand that race was, though significant, just one of the many hurdles I had to clear and that by mentioning it I wasn't playing the card. I anticipated that some would simply see me as just another angry black man. Nevertheless, I decided that if I omitted the race-hurdle experiences, I would be omitting a measurable part of who I am. It would be comparable to asking Ray Charles to write his autobiography or to consult on the making of the movie of his life without mentioning the role blindness played in his life. My objective was to simply share a moving, penetrating message with readers in all walks of life. To that end, I wanted my book to be on your mind long after you put it down.

During my 46 years of breathing, I've learned a great deal about what it takes to be awesome from a number of sources. I've learned from my mother, and from my diverse group of Anchors, Titans, mentors, colleagues, and friends—you'll feel their presence throughout the book.

I've also learned through my numerous experiences while attending schools and universities that were usually predominantly black or predominantly white. I've been the president of a nearly all-black student affinity group in college, and I've been a captain on the football team at that same, nearly all-white, school. Ironically, I've spent my professional life mostly with white people and my personal life (early on) mostly with black people. In essence, I've consistently lived, thrived, and at times barely survived in two unique worlds.

I've been up close and personal with stabbings, muggings, poverty, drugs, roaches, water bugs, and mice as well as with judges, doctors, business owners, corporate executives, lawyers, and professional athletes. It's been some ride! And through this book, I'm going to share my awesome trip.

By reading about my experiences from grade school to the corporate boardroom, you too can move from being average to awesome. I have used the wisdom, perspective, joy, kindness, compassion, hope, solace, and ultimately love of others to move me toward living in an extraordinary way. Because my path to understanding was in no way linear, I have not attempted to create a step-by-step path for you to follow. You will have to discover a path that's right for you. What I have provided is 25 indicators that will help you move toward living a more successful and happy life. You will have to make the positive changes in your life to achieve this worthwhile goal.

Unlike a step-by-step approach, getting from average to awesome in a nonlinear way is in some ways much easier. What if, for example, you cannot complete step 5. Do you just give up or move to step 6? What I invite you to do is use this book as one tool to improve your success and happiness in life. Whether you open up this book to chapter 7, "Make Time, not Excuses, for Your Loved Ones," or chapter 2, "Savor Your Meaningful Moments in Life," you are moving toward awesomeness if you apply what you learn or discover about yourself by reading that chapter.

Regardless of what you do professionally or personally, this book casually and quickly walks and talks you through lessons, keys, anecdotes, experiences, ideas, and practical steps you can take to get the most out of any situation.

Why "awesome"? It's powerful! Its meaning extends so much beyond material wealth, awards, and success. It's more than being the straight-A student or the first to do this or the first to do that. Its meaning goes beyond elaborate titles, too. In a nutshell, being awesome is consistently feeling fulfilled, ecstatic, positive, and energized about yourself and what you do. It's a way of life.

I hope this book moves you to make the life changes you've considered before but put off until now. I hope that it moves you to think more deeply and more consistently about things you've never given much thought to until now. I hope the book asks the appropriate questions and provides the right answers.

If you encounter any skids during your reading, remember what you were taught when learning how to drive: turn into, not away from, the skid. Upon reaching the skid, read and then reread the points that stretch your beliefs and understandings. As Stephen Covey says, "Seek to understand before you seek to be understood." To the best of your ability, attempt to walk in my shoes and the shoes of others who share their experiences in the book. At the very least, ask others for their opinions. You can even email me, and we can discuss any problems you might be having relating these lessons to your own life.

To help you assess and develop your action steps after reading each chapter, I've included a simple exercise that will help you move from average to awesome. Think carefully about your answers, and be honest about where you need help and development. In addition, you should draw inspiration for moving forward by reading the Awesome Advice sidebars and quotes at the beginning of each chapter contributed by my Titans, colleagues, and friends, people just like you from all over the United States, Mexico, and Canada.

This book was originally published in 2005. I have revised it and added new tools and materials to make it even more meaningful and applicable to your own journey to awesome.

I have also provided several bonus chapters with additional stories, tips, and encouragement available for download at www.astd .org/FromAveragetoAwesome. Use these free materials to take more steps toward living an awesome life.

Writing, and then revising, this book was an exceptional experience—at times painful, at times therapeutic, at times exhilarating. I found the entire journey to be extremely rewarding, maturing, and timely. And I could not have done it without you, Mrs. Brodie! Thank you!

Jim Smith Jr.
May 2008

Chapter 1

Build Character by Persevering

> Through joy and pain, patience and persistence, I have mastered the ability to keep myself in a place that gives me inner peace with everyday life changes and trials. Maturity, time, and drive are my best friends.
>
> —LORRAINE HICKS, PHILADELPHIA

uring my corporate training classes, I enjoy telling participants that I attended kindergarten through 12th grade without missing a day of school. Their reactions are nearly always the same: "Oh wow." "No way." "That's impossible." "Awesome." "Your mom must be proud of you." "You're kidding."

I'm extremely proud of this accomplishment! It means as much to me as a gold medal means to an Olympic athlete. My perfect attendance record paved the way for my committed, disciplined, and hardworking approach to life, for my belief that you can work through almost anything if you put your mind to it. After I broke my ankle in the 10th grade during a high school football game, I thought my attendance streak was over. I think I cried more about the streak being over than from the excruciating pain in my ankle. However, the next day, with books in hand and a cast on my leg, I hailed a taxi and went to school. The streak continued!

I also share this little "window into my world" fact because it provides a smooth segue into talking about my Mom, R. Nanci Smith, an African American single parent, who raised her two sons in Philadelphia during the '60s, '70s, and '80s. She mothered us, fathered us, nurtured us, coached us, and at times drove us nuts because of her structured and disciplined approach to living. She guided us to adulthood, teaching us so much about life that I'm just beginning to understand some of her lessons today.

When asked to talk about her two sons, my Mom will ease into the conversation by proudly mentioning that both of us have master's degrees. Education was always important to her.

Her influence on my life's blueprint has been profound; she's been the architect of my values, my rock-firm foundation. She stood on the sidelines, in all kinds of weather, during my Little League, high school, and college games. Her presence was as predictable as that of the cheerleaders, referees, umpires, and goalposts.

She taught me the importance of always being on time and the significance of making a powerful first and lasting impression. She would always say there's more to life than just sports. She inspired the "get involved" spirit in me. To that end, I've lived a life of making it happen rather than watching it happen. She also taught me to always help others, sit in the front row in any class, smile for identification photos, dress my best, be respectful, get up early, make up my bed, keep thorough files, save money, live below my means, take care of myself, and make an impact in whatever I did.

She attended every parent-teacher report card meeting night. She taught me how to balance a checkbook, how to jitterbug, and how to play pinochle (she still is my favorite card partner). But most significantly, she taught me how to reach higher and further and how to recover.

I also tell people about my perfect attendance because it was during those early years that I first learned many lessons about what it takes to be awesome. I learned how to get the most out of whatever I was doing and how to hold on tight even when life was treating me like a dartboard in a crowded tavern. I always sprinted the last lap at the end of practice. I ran my "suicide drills" all-out. I walked the four-mile round-trip to school when our city's public transportation went on strike during the winter months of my freshman year in high school.

My younger brother, Rodney, always tells friends struggling through one of life's tension conventions to "go talk to my brother." You see, Rodney has learned plenty from my bouts with sorrow, injuries, rejection, pain, racial discrimination, corporate politics, failed relationships, and broken promises. He sincerely believes that I'm the poster child for life's ups and downs. "You need to go talk to my brother about that. The same thing happened to him; he'll tell you what to do," he assures friends.

I don't know about all that, but I'm committed to helping people move from OK to outstanding and from average to awesome. I believe we all have talents and gifts. One of my gifts just happens to be that after life smacks me around, I process, savor, shine, and then share. I file, save, retrieve, open, and then print. Recalling my experiences days, months, and years later—after I have thoroughly processed and learned from them—is what really refuels my spirit. My 46-*plus* years have been tumultuous, filled with good guys and bad guys, despair, love, a bunch of "isms," prejudices, competition, stereotypes, graduation, rejection, action, and celebration. I can vividly remember when:

- I was 4 years old and my brother was born; I spoke to my mother on the telephone while she was still in the hospital and I told her to send him back.
- My mother, brother, and I squeezed into telephone booths waiting to catch the bus and trolley cars (on our way to church) during the rainy and frigid winter months.
- Our living room ceiling leaked into the buckets that were placed on the floor every time it rained.
- My father used to say, before commencing the whipping with his black leather strap, that spanking me was going to hurt him more than it was going to hurt me.
- My mother would find the bottles of beer and vodka my father had hidden behind the living room sofa and television set and pour them down the toilet.
- I feared for my life during my commute to and from middle school because of the white neighborhood gang that despised people of color.
- I spent my summers with my Grandmom and Nana in South Philly.
- At age 12, I won my first trophy: the Jayhawks beat Millcreek for the Little League baseball championship.
- As a teenager, I attended the Moore College of Art on a summer internship.
- My parents divorced.
- In high school, I was All-Public in three sports (and honorable mention All-City in two).
- I attended nearly all-white Widener University.
- I dropped an interception in the closing minutes of the Division III National Championship college football game between Widener and the University of Dayton.
- I graduated from Widener with a bachelor of arts degree in English. I was the first in my family to earn a degree (and then couldn't find a job!).

- My mother earned her college degree.
- My high school sweetheart and fiancée ended our five-year relationship one month after I graduated from college.
- I was cut from the professional football teams I tried out for.
- I was married by a justice of the peace, just four months after meeting my wife and less than a year after graduating from college. I also became a stepfather.
- I went through a painful divorce six years later.
- I broke my ankle (twice), ruptured my Achilles tendon, and tore my patellar tendon.
- I received my master's degree from Temple University and was the commencement speaker 13 years later.
- I was first promoted to management.
- I let corporate America mess with my head, my heart, my spirit, and my drive for 14 years.
- I had to drive to work two to three hours each way for three years.
- I spent a day in the hospital waiting for the results of my mother's brain aneurysm surgery.
- I remarried.
- My daughter Daecia was born.
- My best friend's brother, George, died suddenly at age 44 because of a brain aneurysm, leaving behind his wife and four daughters.
- My father died at the age of 59.
- I started using "Jr." in my name.
- I started my own company, JIMPACT Enterprises.
- My second marriage failed.
- My son Ian James was born.

My remembrances could go on, but I think you get the point. That's why my brother sends his friends my way. He believes I can relate to them and their situations, and help them land squarely on their feet. Though I have my own "stuff" to work through at times, I seldom turn down a potential "client" or an opportunity to help turn someone's rotten day around. I get that from my mother, too.

My friend Linda Gillette says she treats every day as a sparkling new adventure. Linda was born and raised in a small community in North Dakota. She says it was a great place to be raised but that magazines and TV stimulated much of her dreaming as a child. She says now, as an adult, her childhood dreams have become a reality. As a business day gets more and more stressful, she just smiles and thinks of where she came from. "Life is good; it is what it is," is one of her favorite quotes.

Consider This: Life without problems is death. You can only have good because of evil, sweet because of sour.

Linda once told me, "We are all going to have hot and cold moments. It's good to embrace both temperatures. I read a book long ago by Norman Vincent Peale. He said a depressed man came up to him after he finished a speech and asked, 'How can I live my life with no problems?' Peale looked at the man and said, 'Die.' Well, the man didn't find the response humorous, but there is truth to the statement. Just understanding this helps me accept my world and in turn keeps me motivated." Linda is incredible!

I remember when my mother, brother, and I moved out of our tiny two-bedroom, one-bath, second-floor apartment on Sansom Street to our first "real house," on Larchwood Avenue in Southwest Philadelphia. We were also moving away from my father. After 13 years of marriage, my mother had grown weary of the alcoholism, lying, disappointments, poor money management, and abuse. We had kept the move a secret from him for fear that he would get violent or try to talk my mother out of leaving. We moved into our new, single-parent home while my dad was at work.

As an 11-year-old, I didn't quite understand the risk my mother was taking. To me, we were just moving, and Dad was not going with us. I thought my parents would eventually reunite— that Dad would find us and things would go back to the way they were, minus the alcohol. He said his affair with the bottle started as a way to warm his insides after spending each workday as a butcher working in frigid, freezer temperatures. He just never ended the relationship with liquor. Mom grew tired of his mistress. They never did get back together. My life story continued. My lessons mounted.

Our plot was now a single-parent family. We were latchkey kids, two boys growing up in our first "house-house," a twin row house in our first interracial neighborhood. We lived right on the outskirts of the University of Pennsylvania campus. I often saw college students of all nationalities going to class and going to parties. I loved this ethnic and racial diversity. Every day Mom rode public transportation to her job in Center City Philadelphia. And every Saturday, she woke us up by yelling, "Jim, Rod, get up! . . . There's work to be done!"

We did not have all the material extras that many of our neighbors had. Other than our home, our 1975 white Chevy Nova was our most valuable asset, and we bought that—our first car—when I was 16. I would use my creativity and resourcefulness to make bats, balls, baskets, and bases from the strangest things in our basement and garage. Today you see basketball courts in the driveway; my brother and I used a puff basketball set to play full court in the dining room. Our foul line was a spot smack in the middle of the floor, directly across from the dining room cabinet doorknob.

AWESOME ADVICE

I was raised in a household considered well below poverty level. My dad was a construction worker, but his hot temper often left the family with little money because he would lose his job frequently. Dad was an alcoholic. Mom, my six siblings, and I often didn't see him for days at a time. We lived in a two-room house with no water, electricity, or plumbing. Yes, we had an outhouse over the hill! It seemed nothing was stable in our lives except the love our parents gave us.

Growing up I often heard, "We don't have the money," and I learned as a child to begin to work for anything I needed or wanted. I decided then that I was going to make it in this world and be the very best I could be. Although I wasn't blessed with wealth and material things, I inherited a big heart, love for all humankind, and an outpouring of love for life.

I've encountered many bumps in the road during my life. I have overcome being a single parent with almost no help from the children's father. I have battled a fight with cancer and won. My father came to live with me last year, and I just recently lost him to cancer. Because I had to take care of my family during and after high school, I have not been able to finish college, but I have worked extremely hard and, with the help of many great people and mentors, I have built my confidence, matured professionally, and made it up the ladder in the largest insurance company in the world. I am now an agent for this company.

I am so proud of my accomplishments! I'm proud of where I came from, and I'm proud of where I've been and where I'm going with my life! The greatest compliment that I receive is when people tell me that I am the most positive and strongest person they know. Strength comes from perseverance and keeping a positive attitude. When you face challenges, keep a smile on your face, a prayer in your heart, and a good attitude.

—Tracie Johnson, Highland Heights, KY

We may have come up short in the "keep up with the Joneses race," but we did have a surplus of love. Mom, with the focus and concentration of a med school student meticulously studying for final exams, was injecting into our lives the discipline, commitment, work ethic, and sense of responsibility that would last all our lives.

Like most kids growing up, I did get into my share of neighborhood fights. Those two-minute tussles were with friends who teased me whenever my mother decided to go out on a date. I guess, for the sake of my physical well-being, that it was a good thing Mom did not date too often. My friends had dads at home, so they were rubbing it in that I did not have one or that I had, in their opinion, too many.

My interests on weekends and during the summer were few and simple: (1) eating TastyKakes, mustard pretzels, and cherry water ices (my favorite snacks); and (2) playing sports outside and inside of the house with Rodney. Our living room and dining room became a multipurpose facility, quickly converted into a baseball field and basketball court while Mom was at work. We used a badminton racket as our bat and a puff basketball as our baseball. For bases, we used old newspapers or couch pillows. Surprisingly, we never broke anything, except our individual records for points scored in an hour or before Mom got home.

Now, as a 46-year-old adult, I can say wow! Mom was courageous. She left her husband during a time when it was extremely rare for a black woman to leave her marriage. She wanted a home, not just a house. She did not care that many of her other friends stayed in their trying marriages. She ignored the black-single-parent, single-woman stereotypes and labels. She had spirit. I often wonder if my Mom's will to find happiness back then paved the way for my not being afraid to leave corporate jobs when I felt unfulfilled and unhappy.

Most people say that you need two incomes to raise a family. Nanci Smith did it extremely well with one. We never thought we were missing out on anything, save the occasional fashion statements and sneakers du jour. Mom was zeroing in on building our character and not going into poverty by spoiling us silly. Our summer vacations were a bus ride to my grandmother's house in South Philly—not to the shore or to a resort. We never missed school, and Mom saw to it that our grades were always in honor roll range.

I believe that the discipline my Mom instilled in me has played a role in my impatience with people who don't like to roll up their sleeves (and then make excuses or play the victim). Mom even went in to work the day after she officially retired (after 40 years of working for the City of Philadelphia). She said that she had several projects she had to wrap up.

Mom has handled her business superbly, always planting the seeds of life into our heads. As a child, the seeds took root inside both my head and my heart, never to be forgotten, and to be shared with so many others. The world, and most specifically our home, was our classroom, and our teacher lived with us. Other people and everyday experiences were our visual aids. I didn't have to take notes. The lessons were powerful and were repeated over and over again.

Moving from Average to Awesome

This chapter is not only about getting past the difficulties and roadblocks we all face in our life journey. It's also about how we process these lessons and use them in a positive way. This exercise will help you move from an average mindset to a more positive and powerful awesome way of living.

First, consider which statement describes how you think about the difficulties and roadblocks you have faced in your own life:

- *Average*: You occasionally reflect on your past but largely dismiss how the past has shaped the person you are today.
- *Awesome*: Life lessons are used to make positive changes in your life. You share what you have learned when you teach, coach, or mentor others.

Now, take some time and consider the questions below. Respond to the questions and be sure to explain your answers. Finally, rate yourself on your progress. If you are currently average, say so (A). If you feel you deserve an awesome rating, indicate that as well (AW). If you are neither average nor awesome, but working toward being awesome, just write W.

Getting to Awesome

Key questions	Your response and explanation	Rating
Do you effectively use your past to inform and guide the decisions you make today?		
What roadblocks and difficulties have you faced in life and how did you overcome them?		
When was the last time you used the lessons from your own life to help someone else?		

Rate your progress: average (A), awesome (AW), or working toward awesome (W).

Chapter 2

Savor Your Meaningful Moments in Life

What I am beginning to learn at the age 53 is how to live in the moment—how to pause . . . look about . . . as I walk to the bank, drive my beautiful children to school, even as I put out the garbage in the fresh early hours of the morning. I think about the incredible natural and spiritual beauty that surrounds me. I look, I feel, I appreciate, and I'm thankful.

—JUDY CHAPMAN, TORONTO

I started writing this chapter in my head in December 1981. I resumed writing it nearly 20 years later, in September 2001, as my wife (at the time), Pat, and I were driving to Pittsburgh to attend the wedding of my friends Becky and Nick.

Unlike many of the out-of-towners who attended the nuptials, we opted to drive to Pittsburgh from New Jersey rather than fly. As a motivational speaker, trainer, and consultant, I'm a frequent flier and I see more airports than Disney World sees children during the summertime. So spending six hours in our car multitasking, playing catch-up with Pat, listening to Marvin Gaye and Tammi Terrell, Luther Vandross, Anita Baker, Regina Belle, Patti LaBelle, Babyface, and Stevie Wonder, while preparing for an upcoming motivational workshop, appealed to me more than the prospect of facing long lines and privacy-invading security checks at another airport.

I was in multitasking mania as I drove, listening to *Babyface Unplugged*, searching deep inside my heart and mind for key motivational points to make during my upcoming speaking engagement. I wanted this program to rank as one of my best of all time, because I would be presenting it to a former employer. (You always want the ex to see you at your best.)

I continued to look out the window, admiring the effect the sun was having on the beautiful hillsides, searching for a clever way to capture the spirit of my favorite Benjamin E. Mays poem during my presentation:

> I have only just a minute,
> only sixty seconds in it,
> forced upon me—can't refuse it,
> didn't seek it, didn't choose it.
> But it's up to me to use it.
> I must suffer if I lose it.
> Give account if I abuse it.
> Just a tiny little minute—
> but eternity is in it.

I looked over to Pat and said, "I wish I had the camera." Our 35-millimeter was resting in the trunk with all the other wedding stuff. I then got on my soapbox: "There are so many things that happen to us each day, so many moments, so many important times. . . . We never spend time just capturing the moment or the feeling. . . . We let the moment whisk right by. It's a shame! We rush through life!"

We need to savor our moments.

"We don't even honor the moments we have when we're talking one-to-one," I continued. "There's always the cellphone, the pager, or some other distraction competing for—and winning—our attention. We should take cameras with us all the time so we can always take pictures of our significant moments right away!"

Then it hit me! That was the point I was going to make at the workshop! That was the point I was going to drive home: to savor your moments! And, at that very moment, the words of Babyface glided from the car stereo, ". . . gone too soon." Little did I know then that I would never give that speech to my former client. The speech was canceled. It was scheduled for September 11.

I guess I developed this "savoring" sense when my mother, brother, and I began our journey together alone without my Dad. We truly appreciated the times we had—Nanci and her two boys. We protected each other. We visited relatives together. We went to amusement parks together, and we worked on and cleaned the house together. We had a number of deep family discussions. I loved those times!

Consider This: "And in the end, it's not the years in your life that count. It's the life in your years." —Abraham Lincoln

More than 20 years ago, when I began writing this chapter in my head, I knelt in the middle of the field in Phenix City, Alabama, at the conclusion of the Amos Alonzo Stagg Bowl game (the National Championship for NCAA Division III football), which my team had won. I looked to the sky, feeling and listening to everything that was going on around me. The sun seemed to be singing, "Celebrate good times, come on . . ." and my teammates were going crazy. They were high-fiving, belly bumping, and giving each other Gatorade showers. Our fans were also exuberant. I was the only one, several yards away, by myself silently reveling, processing, so in the moment. I wasn't being antisocial. I was savoring my moment.

Widener University had just beaten the University of Dayton 17–10 for the Division III National Football Championship. I would get a championship ring, celebrations back on campus, an all-night, floor-shaking party at the tiny Black Student Union house, and a life lesson that I would recall 20 years later.

I don't know what motivated me not to immediately join in all the on-field frivolity at the time. Maybe I was thinking about the two playoff losses that had ended our seasons during my freshman and sophomore years. Maybe I was thinking of our mind-numbing 28–24 loss to Dayton (we were winning 24–0 at halftime) in the playoffs the previous season. Maybe I was thinking about the hundreds of thousands of college athletes, male and female, who never win a national championship. Maybe I was thinking about the fact that I would be the first student-athlete from my high school, University City, to ever win a college championship. Maybe I was thinking about the national championship ring that I was going to wear for the rest of my life. Maybe I was thinking that this would be as close as I'd ever come to playing in the Super Bowl. Or maybe I was just thinking about the magnitude of our accomplishment, especially because we had been losing 10–0 at halftime. I think the answer is all the above.

I remember exactly what I was feeling as I looked at the grass, looked at the people jumping around, looked at the dejected faces of the Dayton players and fans, and looked to my God to thank him for everything he'd done for me. I eventually joined the on-field hysteria, but for those first few minutes, I was having a moment—savoring my special moment, a moment that I will never forget.

How are you doing right now in savoring your moments?

We live and work in a society where we are always in a hurry. We rush as we get dressed in the morning. We rush to work. We rush to meetings. We rush to the bathroom. We rush home and we rush our dinner down our throats. We rush conversations with friends and loved ones. We rush to get promoted and we rush to judgment. Have you ever wanted someone to just cut to the chase rather than providing you with all the supporting details?

I can recall my first promotion to a management job in corporate America. I had been counting the days. According to my personal Jim Smith file, I did what I thought I needed to do. I had my bachelor's degree (and was working on my master's), and I had put in my time, paid my dues, moved laterally to position myself for promotion, and worked extremely diligently for six very taxing but beneficial years. Each year had seemed like a decade whenever one of my department colleagues—the friends with whom I had joined the organization and who had been my teammates in intercompany sports leagues—was promoted. What a bittersweet taste! Of course I was thrilled for them— we ate lunch together every day; we played fantasy football together; we were like a family during and after work. But, at the same time, I was miffed. For some reason that was never clearly explained to me, my corporate ladder just seemed steeper, more slippery, and more difficult to climb than theirs. We were all bright, all professional, all personable, and all diligent and competent workers. We even partnered on many projects. There was one major difference however: our race. I did not want to believe that race played a factor. I just wanted, yet never received, a thorough explanation. I kept asking management for clarification. I wanted to win, not wilt.

I was the next to the last of our "work family" to get promoted to management. The last to join the management ranks was my buddy Skip. Skip's black, too.

When my boss first made the announcement during a quickly called division meeting, handing me the promotion envelope with everyone anxiously standing outside her office, I thanked her and quickly excused myself from the celebration. I retreated to my own office to savor my moment. I closed the door and had a private celebration filled with tears and prayers. I thought to myself, "I did it! I did it! Finally, I did it!"

As word of my promotion spread, a phenomenon occurred that made this promotion even more special: I was treated like some sort of a messiah by many of the other blacks in the organization. I felt like I was Dr. Martin Luther King Jr., Muhammad Ali, Tom Joyner, and Tavis Smiley rolled into one when, as I walked through the halls, I was greeted with an enthusiastic "thank you" or "don't forget me" or "about time they promoted one of us to management."

Peter Dailey, one of my mentors at the time, took me to lunch to celebrate my promotion. He was class personified: brilliant, funny, clever, soft-spoken, and well dressed. I loved watching him with people. I asked him to be my mentor initially because my other mentor, Sylvia Garvin, a black woman, told me that if I wanted to learn many of the tricks of the game called corporate America, I would need a white male mentor. She believed that white males had influence, information, and—with that—the power. Peter was white.

Although I wish that I had first asked Peter to be my mentor because I thought he was the best person for the job and because I marveled at how he carried himself, rather than using his race as the most determining factor, I benefited from his wisdom and thoroughness nonetheless. During our mentoring relationship, Peter and I learned plenty about each other.

However, I would shortly learn something else that would completely blow me away. Sylvia provided that lesson, too. She told me that Peter wasn't white enough. "What's white enough?" I thought.

She believed that Peter, who was also a member of the organization's professional affinity group for minorities, was blacker than many of the other black people in the company (that is, he had a lot of soul in his stroll, his approach to life, and in his spirit). She encouraged me to maintain my relationship with Peter, but she said that if I was truly serious about spreading my corporate wings, I would need mentoring from a seasoned white male leader—one who was sharp, tough, aggressive, rigid, old-fashioned, and averse to the corporate love affair that organizations had with diversity initiatives, and who also had an exclusive membership in the "good old boys" club. She believed that this type of mentor, who arguably would be difficult to enlist, could help open the club doors that had seemed cemented, bolted, and padlocked shut to me before. I did find such mentors, and more doors were opened. But that's another story, for another day, perhaps another book.

During my promotion-celebration lunch, Peter reminded me of the significance of savoring your moments. He told me to always remember how I felt right at that very moment. He said the feeling would help me during times when I needed a pick-me-up. Because of Peter, I save thank-you notes and cards that people send me, and I also record and save the thank-you voicemails that I receive. I've become a moment-savoring machine. Peter also pushed my reward-yourself snowball down the hill. I talk about that more in my bonus chapter entitled "Treat Yourself as Special—Wow Yourself" available for free download at www.astd.org/FromAverage toAwesome. (Check out this and other bonus material online.) Thank you, Peter. File, save.

We really should take a camera along, figuratively and literally, everywhere we go. How many times have you heard someone say, "Man, I wish I had my camera!"? Sure, we have our cameras poised and ready during graduations, weddings, holidays, anniversaries, births, and family reunions. But is that it? Are those the only times where we create or have wonderful memories?

What moments have you had today? How about this month? This year? December 31 is not the only time for personal reflection!

Not too long ago, I was having a rather poignant conversation with my good friend Aileen. We were talking about making the most of one's time, and she began to tell me about "that lady on the plane." My interest was piqued, and I asked her to continue with her story.

Aileen said that she was flying home after a business trip and brief visit with some old friends. She said she was feeling disappointed that the visit was so brief, and that her friends, who she had not seen for some time, were super busy and couldn't spend the time together that they had anticipated. She said the woman sitting next to her picked up on Aileen's melancholy mood and asked what was wrong. Aileen briefly told her what was troubling her but was surprised and forever changed with "the lady's" response.

"The lady on the plane" said that she had just finished visiting her daughter, who was in the military. She explained that her daughter had scheduled that particular week off so that they could spend quality time together; they only saw each other twice a year. The lady said that she had eagerly flown out to Los Angeles only to find out, upon her arrival, that her daughter had been called to work. Aileen said how sorry she was to hear that the lady's vacation had been ruined. In response the lady said, "It wasn't ruined, . . . although the time we had was limited, I was happy just being in LA, knowing that when my daughter came home from work, I would be there. Just to know that I was sharing her space for one week was enough for me."

Through her anecdote, the lady told Aileen that she savored her moments with her daughter. She said that they laugh, smile, and make the most of every moment they have together.

Aileen absorbed the lesson and vowed to change her perspective. Humbly and candidly, she acknowledged that it wasn't going to be easy but that she was going to do it. She said that she was

AWESOME ADVICE

Being mostly an "up" person, I believe I remain that way by enjoying the people around me, actually the world around me. I wake up every day happy to be given another day to surround myself with beautiful scenery and people I love and care about. Keeping a positive attitude seems to draw and inspire positive results.

Sure, there are down times, but during those times, I always think to myself, "This too shall pass." That little phrase has gotten me through many rough periods by helping me to remember that other "down" times passed and, in an entire lifetime, only lasted for a very short time before all was well again.

—Barb Kompelein, Edina, MN

going to tell all her friends, and other special people in her life, how great it was to see them, to be with them and how much richer her life was as a result of knowing them. "The lady on the plane"—a person, a moment my friend will savor for a long time.

My friend Laura Bruner earned her certification in "moment savoring" last year. She recently shared with me the experience that changed her forever. "Jim, last year I survived an automobile accident that changed my approach to life," she began. "My little sports car and three other cars were totaled in the crash. As I careened into oncoming highway traffic, I quietly closed my eyes because I believed I was living my last moments on Earth. Fortunately, however, when I opened my eyes, I realized that rescue workers would soon have me out of my crushed car and on the way to the emergency room. I did get pretty banged up, but I lived. I have stopped throwing the present away. I treasure life and make sure I send lots of thank-you notes!"

As I put the bow on this chapter, I couldn't help but think of the many moments that have shaped my life. They have taken permanent residence in my mind. I can't wait to have more. I'll savor them, too. *How are you doing right now in savoring your moments?*

Moving from Average to Awesome

This chapter is not only about savoring the good times we experience. It's also about how we need to discern when we are, indeed, having one of those magical moments. This exercise will help you move from an average mindset to a more positive and powerful awesome way of living.

First, consider which statement describes how you think about capturing, framing, and revisiting the exceptional, unexpected, and poignant moments that occur in your life:

- *Average:* You remember to take your physical camera along to capture special moments on holidays and special occasions.

- *Awesome:* You routinely take your mental *and* physical camera along to capture your special, significant, planned and unplanned moments. You share your moments with others. You keep a daily journal, even if it's just a few lines to keep those memories alive. You save voicemails from your favorite people. You're not in a hurry!

Now, take some time and consider the questions below. Respond to the questions and be sure to explain your answers. Finally, rate yourself on your progress. If you are currently average, say so (A). If you feel you deserve an awesome rating, indicate that as well (AW). If you are neither average nor awesome but working toward being awesome, just write W.

Getting to Awesome

Key questions	Your response and explanation	Rating
Are capturing the magical times in your life important to you?		
Do you rely on others to capture your experiences in writing or on video/film?		
Do you rush through your days, seldom taking a timeout to rest or to soak in all that you've accomplished? Is it always what's next on your "to do" list?		

Rate your progress: average (A), awesome (AW), or working toward awesome (W).

Chapter 3

Remember Your Titans

Awesomeness comes from my having a family, mentors, co-workers, and cheerleaders who are supportive and who demonstrate that success doesn't have to mean sacrifice. They applaud my wins and nudge me back into the game after a defeat.

—SHERYL B. CRAUN, SALEM, NH

'm not the average moviegoer. I don't attend premieres, and I love standing in long lines about as much I'd enjoy drinking a 32-ounce jar of that hot yellow Chinese mustard. Lately, the only movies I've gone to see, thanks to my daughter Daecia, have had a Disney flavor: *Flicka*, *The Greatest Game Ever Played*, *Dreamer*, *August Rush*, *No Reservations*, and *Akeelah and the Bee*. In fact, with my busy schedule, I usually wait for movies to make it to cable. There, without the interruptions of boisterous laughs and people standing to make bathroom, Raisinettes, and popcorn runs, I can comfortably watch movies from my couch.

However, a couple of years ago I saw a movie that will rate as one of my top five movies of all time.

On a flight from Philadelphia to Phoenix, I was very pleasantly surprised, intrigued, and uplifted by the movie selected. I was treated to *Remember the Titans*. If you haven't seen it, rent it. Then buy it! Fast!

When *Titans* first came out in theaters, I didn't break my neck or my schedule to go to see it. Typical Disney sports movie, I thought. The for-children-only movie, I believed, would have a little drama, provoke a few tears, then conclude with a happy ending. There would be happy good guys and happy bad guys, happy pets, happy music, and happy credits. Maybe some pixie dust and animation? Boy, was I wrong. I was moved, touched, changed, and reminded. I cried. I laughed. I remembered. I sat motionless at the end.

Titans, a true story, quickly took me back to my youth, my years of playing Little League football for YGS (Young Great Society), for University City High School in West Philadelphia, and for Widener University in college.

In this true story, Denzel Washington plays Herman Boone, an embattled, drill-sergeant-tough, black football coach in a 1971 racially divided neighborhood, school district, and football program. The T. C. Williams High School Titans are his black and white student-athletes who learn, through Boone and his white assistant head coach, Bill Yost (played by Will Patton), about football execution, building relationships, team chemistry, racial inequities, teamwork, and love. During these tough-love, no-pain/no-gain moments, Boone has to contend with the white town folks who want him ousted as head coach and the white referees who collude in attempts to steal the Titans' moral and on-field victories.

Boone's minefields also include building a relationship with Yost, a popular, respected, and legendary town favorite who had been the team's head coach before equal opportunity legislation led to Boone's replacing him. Before the movie concludes, they all come together, save some of the neighborhood folks, to form an impenetrable bond.

Who are your Titans? Who are the people who always have your best interests at the forefront of their minds? Who are the people who always have your back? Who are the people who call you just to say they care? Who are the people who have left indelible marks on your life? Who are the people who love you in spite of the fact that you talk with food in your mouth or that you never return their calls in a timely manner?

Do your Titans mean a great deal to you? Really? If so, then why don't you check in with them more often? Why don't you drop them a line to let them know that you care? Why don't you send them more thank-you notes? It's one of the mysteries in life that we always name streets or buildings after people once they have passed away.

My Titans have played pivotal roles in both my personal and professional lives. Descriptions? Just think diversity.

As a teenager, and then as a college student, I formed a team of Titans composed of mostly athletic coaches. Because my parents were divorced and I did not have a consistent father figure in my life, I really latched onto the men who led my athletic teams. Only one of those men was black (Mr. Sam); most of my Titans/coaches/dads (they were one and the same) were Jewish men, namely Sonny Elia (my high school junior varsity baseball and basketball coach) and Steve Kane (my high school varsity basketball coach).

We had, and still have, AWESOME relationships. I can still recall during my freshman and sophomore years in college telephoning Steve from my dormitory, fuming about how I thought the football coaches were treating me unfairly. Ironically, after my final year on the team, one of those coaches apologized to me for

AWESOME
ADVICE

I would not be where I am today without the unconditional love and support of my soul mate, my best friend, my husband. His continual belief in my talents has helped me to make the sacrifice I may not have wanted to make but which ultimately paid off for me, personally and professionally.

His willingness to keep the home fires burning and spend many days alone while I have been on the road is what has helped me face those countless nights in Holiday Inns. I know that he will always be there for me, encouraging, listening, laughing, and holding me. His eagerness to be both mom and dad when needed is what has helped me be anything but average.

He always thinks I am awesome, even when I don't feel like it.

—Priscilla Shumway, Isle of Palms, SC

not playing me more, sooner. Imagine my white Titan/coach/dad doing his best to console me and offer solutions for my deep beliefs that favoritism and racism were also opponents I had to tackle.

Another one of my Titans, my great grandmother Carrie Bryant, recently passed away at the age of 97. She practically raised me during my early teenage years when I spent many of my summers at her three-story South Philadelphia home. She used to wear me out playing checkers and pinochle. Grandmom is my heart. I remember all the times we played checkers for pennies and she cleaned my clock. She would win every one of my tired little pennies. The routine was the same. She would crush me at penny checkers. I would fight back tears, then head down the third-floor steps back to the first floor. Before I got too far, she would call me back, give me back my pennies, and tell me to practice before I challenged her again. That was Grandmom.

She taught me about responsibility, commitment, caring, and personal empowerment. Some of my favorite memories from those summers include playing hide-and-go-seek, basketball, half-ball, deadblock, and tops, riding my bike, and doing chores for "Grams." I really enjoyed washing dishes because Grams loved a clean kitchen. For more than 50 years, she traveled up and down the three stories with one single objective: to put out the family fires on the first and second floors that threatened to pull our dysfunctional family further apart.

Consider This: "Angels fly high because they take themselves lightly."
—G. K. Chesterton

During our wedding reception 14 years ago, my ex-wife and I made sure we selected an extra-long song (Taylor Dayne's extended version of "I'll Always Love You" was the choice) during the family introductions. We wanted to make sure Grandmom had sufficient time to walk down the aisle to her seat so that everyone could see and marvel at the woman, and feel the strength that had enabled her to keep our family together. Before the wedding, I kept asking her if she was going to be there. She would just calmly smile and say, "God willing, Jimmy, I'll be there." She was an incredible Titan!

Kathy Cook was my manager for three years at one of my corporate stops. This five-foot, fast-walking and fast-talking, charismatic woman taught me more about professionalism in the three years I reported to her than I had learned in the previous nine. She always provided the appropriate feedback (a timely anecdote, coaching conversation, hug, handshake, or slap on the wrist). She was savvy. She was strategic. She was tough. She was brilliant. She knew how to manage and how to motivate people. She taught me about not taking on bad business.

I remember wanting to help lead our organization's diversity initiative when I came on board. Kathy had hired me to coach, develop, and train supervisors and managers. Because I had done an enormous amount of diversity work at my previous job, I thought this would be a sensational way to make an immediate impact at the company. Kathy said "Absolutely not!" She said, "Jim, there will be time later for you to do diversity work here. I want people to get to know you as a person and to see your management development abilities and talents—not just see another black man leading another diversity council. I don't want them to avoid you. I want them to embrace you. I want you to build allies."

I did not realize it right away, but like my mother's protective lesson about always appearing approachable and smiling, Kathy's plan seemed to me to be strategic and protective but somehow unfair. I remember thinking, "What kind of world are we living in when a manager believes she has to divert an employee's interest to another assignment because of the stereotypes, beliefs, attitudes, and mindsets that go along with being a person of color in a particular management position?"

Consider the loss. The company lost a valuable diversity resource. I lost a valuable opportunity to assist the organization by utilizing my diversity skills, resources, experiences, and talents—all in the name of perceived bias and prejudices.

At any rate, three years and an Award of Excellence later, Kathy asked me if I was ready to get back into the diversity business. I had built a solid track record, and there were plenty of opportunities brewing with my name written on many of them. I declined any large role. I told her that if we could connect the diversity responsibilities within my new role as an organizational effectiveness consultant, I would do it. And we did—successfully. Consider my gain.

I left the organization shortly after that. During my surprise going-away party (of course Kathy orchestrated the entire event), I was exuberant yet torn. I loved what my new job offered, but I would be leaving my coach, my boss, my mentor, my Titan, and my friend, Kathy Cook. As the silverware began to clink the glasses, and choruses of "speech, speech, speech" began to mount, I walked to the front of the room. With Kathy at my side, I began to thank everyone for being awesome colleagues and teammates. When I began to thank Kathy, I turned to look at my Titan, and it was sob city. During my "the way we were speech," I cried like a toddler whose favorite ball had just rolled into the sewer.

Question. Do you routinely take your Titans for granted? What's that about? I am where I am today because of my Titans.

We spend more time with our "Titanics," the people who bring us down and intentionally or unintentionally try to sink us, than we do with our Titans. Why?

Titans are consistent and more dependable than the person who delivers your mail. They help you to give birth to your greatness or rediscover it. Through their words and their actions, they provide immeasurable support. Just when you're feeling drained from drama or whipped from worry, they give you a call out of the blue or send you a note to remind you how important you are to them. So call them more often. Visit them more often. Email them more often. Text (SMS) them more often. Remember your Titans!

Moving from Average to Awesome

This chapter is not only about remembering your Titans. It's also about how you respond to the incredible advice and life lessons they provide for you. This exercise will help you move from an average mindset to a more positive and powerful awesome way of living.

First, consider which statement describes how you think about creating more time and opportunities for your Titans:

- **Average:** You check in with your Titans every now and then for advice and guidance.
- **Awesome:** You consistently make your Titans a part of your life. You communicate with them whenever you can to remind them that they indeed do make a difference. You'll pick up the phone right now and call one of your Titans!

Now, take some time and consider the questions below. Respond to the questions, and be sure to explain your answers. Finally, rate yourself on your progress. If you are currently average, say so (A). If you feel you deserve an awesome rating, indicate that as well (AW). If you are neither average nor awesome but working toward being awesome, just write W.

Getting to Awesome

Key questions	Your response and explanation	Rating
Are your Titans surprised to hear from you when you check in? Do you spend more time with your Titans or Titanics?		
Do you only check in with your Titans when you want something?		
Do your find yourself routinely ignoring the advice you receive from your Titans, choosing instead to do things your own way?		

Rate your progress: average (A), awesome (AW), or working toward awesome (W).

Chapter 4

Don't Go to Pity Parties

> I won't allow myself to regress to past failures unless it is to analyze how I could have done them differently or better. I live each day to the fullest. I'd rather burn out than rust out. Life is too short to spend it complaining. I enjoy living!
>
> —ROBERTA SALISBURY, HINCKLEY, ME

Have you ever had a pity party? Come on. You know, those parties where you sit around moaning and groaning, heaving and grieving, crying and complaining, whining and worrying about some misfortune that has happened to you—and then not doing anything about it. I've had my share!

Being raised in a single-parent family did not trigger them; nor did my family's lack of money and lack of material wealth. I was challenged and at times frustrated, yet strengthened, time after time when I attended mostly white schools. I got used to being the only black person. Those realities were character-building and developmental; they prepared me for the real world.

I guess what did prompt my first significant pity party was the unexpected moment when Benae, my high school sweetheart (and fiancée), abruptly ended our relationship shortly after I graduated from college. To say I was devastated is an understatement.

We started dating when we were in high school. I was a senior and she was a junior. I was captain of the football, baseball, and basketball teams and she was captain of the cheerleading squad. Everyone in our circle of friends believed that Smitty and Nay were going to be together until death did us part. We often kidded each other about designing the interior of our home using our black-and-gold high school colors.

Benae even joined me at Widener for college. She left after two years to finish school in Philadelphia, but our relationship continued to flourish. We got engaged during the second semester of my senior year. Our relationship was the stuff Paramount and Columbia Pictures crave—except that our ending was as unexpected and as sudden as Magic Johnson's initial announcement that he was retiring from playing professional basketball for the Los Angeles Lakers because he was HIV-positive.

Shortly after I graduated from college, Benae said (and I'm sure that I'm not the only male who abhors this phrase), "This isn't working for me, but we can still be friends." She said that she wanted to grow and to start seeing other people; and that if we were meant to be, we would get together again at some point. I was crushed. My fairy tale relationship was over. The football player and the cheerleader was now a painful memory. For the rest of the summer and right through the fall, I had one long, exasperating pity party. Every song on the radio, every show on television, and every movie I went to see to take my mind off Benae reminded me of our yesterdays.

After that, the parties started to occur more often than reruns on Nick at Nite. One would think I was a pity party animal.

During the Benae pity party, other parties started occurring simultaneously. The music became deafening. The USFL Philadelphia Stars cut me—and my professional football hopes—three months after the Benae breakup. Sitting in the stands teary-eyed, knowing that I would never again hear the crowd's roar or that I would never feel the rush of adrenaline that competitive sport creates was a tough pill to swallow. In addition, I had ongoing gainful unemployment mini-pity-parties after months of unsuccessfully trying to turn my English degree into a career.

Actually, my ongoing Benae pity parties affected me more than I realized. I got married by a justice of the peace eight months after Benae and I went our separate ways. I had known my wife for just four months, having met her at a friend's wedding on New Year's Eve 1983. We exchanged our vows four months later on April 28, 1984. I also became her 4-year-old son's stepfather. My rationale: I went from not having anyone to love to now having two people to wrap my arms around. Our union lasted six maturing, tumultuous, and character-building years.

Coincidentally, Benae married four months after I did. I'm certain I saw her wedding party drive by my home as I sat on my front porch that August afternoon. Seeing them took me back to the "we can just be friends" breakup day. Ouch!

During my early years in corporate America, I had a pity party nearly every time someone in my department whom I deemed less deserving received a promotion instead of me. I wasn't used to being bypassed. It was humbling and frustrating. I can't say that I ever got used to it. My ex-wife would always say, ". . . then do something about it!" In fact, that *was* my modus operandi for every other challenge in my life, but this was different. This felt more paralyzing. So whenever I believed I was encountering institutional racism, classism, nepotism, bias, stereotypes, and the like, if you brought the music, I would bring the resentment, the rage, and the resistance. If

I wasn't partying alone, I hosted pity parties with other mournful partygoers.

Our pity parties had a familiar routine: Share your dilemma, get agreement that it wasn't your fault, share what you were or were not going to do as a result, then close your remarks with "See, . . . that's why it doesn't make a difference if you. . . ." Some of those parties were classic. We all ordered all we could from that "whine list of life."

I remember when I worked for my first major company and my good friend Skip and I would sit in my car after work for hours, pity partying about yet another white guy from our inner circle of friends who had gotten a promotion over us. Ironically, it always rained on those days. I can still see the windshield wipers slowly going back and forth, back and forth, and back and forth. They made a quirky noise. Rather than hearing squish, squish, squish, squish, I heard, as the wipers went back and forth, "left out again, left out again, left out again." Skip and I felt helpless, and we were livid. At times I wanted to put my fist through the window. At times I wanted to quit. I didn't care that I did not have another job to go to.

We also moved into depression. After questioning ourselves, our work habits, and our performance, we took dead aim at the organization. I always woke up from those pity parties with horrible "I still work there" hangovers. Trying to come up with personal solutions for systemic problems was gut-wrenching.

My other hangovers were the aftermath of dwelling on no-win issues, like "Why me?" or "What could have/should have been" or "It hurts so much." I was always an overachiever. I wanted the A-plus. I was in the National Honor Society in high school. I was a captain on every athletic team, every level, that I played for. I more than held my own in spite of the racial imbalances of several of my schools. I was accustomed to shaking off the dust and getting back up. I welcomed and weathered the storms. Nothing could break

my spirit. But, for the first five or six years after college graduation, I wavered. Two failed relationships and corporate "play-with-
your-head" games really rocked my personal belief system.

During my divorce, I had an epiphany: sometimes life isn't
hard—we make it hard. Sure, life isn't always going to be a pictur-
esque day in Aruba, but it's what you do *after* you get the run in
your pantyhose, the shopping cart in the back of the ankle, or the
empty gas tank in the middle of nowhere that counts.

Consider This: "What lies behind us and
what lies before us are tiny matters
compared to what lies within us."
—Ralph Waldo Emerson

Pity parties only linger if you let them linger. I cannot say
what the exact trigger was, but sometime in the midst of all my
divorce muck, I decided that in the future, when things looked
bleak, I would get mad, get sad, get better, and then get busy. I felt
empowered! I still feel empowered!

Please don't think I'm insensitive. I do understand that life is
sometimes painful. Unforeseen circumstances seemingly occur as
often as delayed flights. The sting of a loved one's death can last
for what seems like forever. And yes, sometimes you have to have
that sorrowful, "it-hurts-all-over" cry. But with time, we have to
move on. Learn from the experience, file it, save it, but move on.
Burn the negative tapes. Turn off the pity party soundtracks. Turn
on the full-steam-ahead adrenaline. As Søren Kierkegaard said,
"Life can only be understood backwards, but it must be lived
forwards."

My friend Tony Spann has been like a second brother since
we met in second grade at the Henry C. Lee Elementary School's

AWESOME
ADVICE

My mom once told me (and she had an extremely difficult time as a single parent raising my brother and me), "What other choice do I have—to be negative? How would that help me with all that I have on my plate? It serves no purpose!"

Those words stay with me when I start to think or speak negatively. We all have to vent our frustrations at times, and sometimes just the release will help you get past the negative feelings, allowing you to focus on the positive.

My motto is: Release it, and then move on! Don't ignore it, or it will resurface. Purge it. Do whatever it takes, but make sure it's gone!

—Lisa Marzullo, Chicago

little red schoolhouse in 1967. With the last names "Smith" and "Spann," we sat next to each other in many classes during that memorable year and those that followed. My family became his extended family and vice versa. His oldest brother, George, filled in as my "voice of wisdom" and "big brother" during my teenage and early adult years.

When Tony saw his mother's phone number on his pager late one evening at his Chicago home, he had a sinking feeling that she hadn't called just for a trivial chat or a routine check-in. He sensed that something terrible had occurred. When he returned the call, he braced himself, but not adequately.

George had died.

"Never in my wildest dreams did I think my mother's news would be so devastating," Tony told me. "I found myself experiencing feelings that I had never experienced before. I found myself enraged, bewildered, depressed, deeply saddened, and overwhelmed by grief. George was my brother and my confidant, as well as my father figure. Losing him was catastrophic for me. I was numb for days. Simultaneously, as if functioning in two parallel universes, I became inspired to get my family through this depressing period of our collective lives. I began to see things in a different, clearer light. I was instrumental in consoling everyone, and my immediate focus switched to playing a significant role in all our family matters leading up to the day of his funeral and for the first two years after his death. I never actually gave myself the opportunity to grieve until I felt that everyone in my immediate family, as well as his widow and four daughters, had reached a point where they could function relatively 'normally' under the circumstances. His memory and spirit were guiding me, motivating me to provide emotional, financial, and physical support to everyone. The other amazing thing that occurred was that I became acutely aware of my mortality."

"This realization moved me to pursue everything with renewed vigor and dedication. I felt invincible; it was as if all of George's skills, abilities, and talents had merged with mine. My desire to enrich my family members' lives in every possible way became my preoccupation. I talked about him in the present tense, and I shared every memory I had with anyone who would listen."

"James, as a result of George's death," Tony continued, "I believe that I am more complete; my confidence is as high as ever, and I believe that I can and will achieve anything my heart desires. He is still my inspiration; his memory helps me to keep things in perspective. I feel like the phoenix, coming out of the ashes, as if reborn, to live a self-fulfilling prophecy."

I know a number of individuals who have given in to life's inequities and kicks in the teeth. They have time-shares in Victimville. Their perception of the world never changes. Their perception of themselves never changes. Their favorite quote is "If it is to be, don't look at me." As a result, I've come to believe that we get what we expect, not what we want. We get what we are. Our external world is significantly affected by our internal world. Consequently, when we expect negative things are going to happen, because negative thoughts are running recklessly through our minds, they usually do.

It's easy to throw a pity party. It's easy to wallow in "Oh well, I can't do anything about it." It's easy to blame the system or blame the boss. Remember that awesome people, in the throes of drama, pain, unfairness, and uncertainty, are able to get mad, get sad, get better, and then get busy. Today, Tony is doing incredibly well. He is still on a mission. George's memory is his bridge to greatness, not his roadblock. When George died, Tony got mad, got sad, then eventually got better. And he stays busy, consistently striving toward awesome.

Moving from Average to Awesome

This chapter is not only about being resilient and bouncing back. It's also about the impact and lingering effects pity parties can have. This exercise will help you move from an average mindset to a more positive and powerful awesome way of living.

First, consider which statement describes how you think about your response to setbacks:

- **Average:** You hold on to negative feelings and let those feelings affect the decisions you make.
- **Awesome:** You learn from unfortunate situations and occurrences and let those times become catalysts for continued personal growth, desire, development, discipline, determination, and strength.

Now, take some time and consider the questions below. Respond to the questions, and be sure to explain your answers. Finally, rate yourself on your progress. If you are currently average, say so (A). If you feel you deserve an awesome rating, indicate that as well (AW). If you are neither average nor awesome but working toward being awesome, just write W.

Getting to Awesome

Key questions	Your response and explanation	Rating
When was the last time you played the victim?		
Do you overreact and get defensive when you are questioned about your role in what happened?		

continued on next page

continued from the previous page

Key questions	Your response and explanation	Rating
What do you do to maintain your composure and positive mindset when things are not going as you would like?		

Rate your progress: average (A), awesome (AW), or working toward awesome (W).

Chapter 5

Expect an Awesome Day!

> I have regular practices that help me generate positive energy. I meditate, exercise, journal, read, and write a "grateful list" every day.
>
> —DELORIS DAVIS, PHILADELPHIA

My cubicle in the office building was directly adjacent to a massive, long tinted window overlooking the employee parking lot. The window reminded me of one that you would look through to observe sea life at the Camden or Baltimore aquariums. Because the window was tinted, it gave me a private, early-morning view of my co-workers' daily regimens—slowly emerging from their cars, reluctantly trudging to their nine-to-fives. They usually appeared somber, fatigued, frustrated, wearing sour expressions.

Once inside, some of them, with attitudes to match their facial expressions, would stagger to the cafeteria to satisfy their morning coffee addiction and hunger pangs. My typically "good morning" greetings were usually met with "What's so good about it?" "Don't talk to me until I get my coffee!" "Jim, what are you so happy about? People like you really annoy me." "You know I'm not a morning person. . . . I'll call you later."

These people were doing their prosecutorial best to argue for an absolutely pitiful morning. They would object to any motions for smiles and laughter. And they were successful, winning their "bad morning" cases day after day.

How do you start each day?

The morning is an opportune time for programming your subconscious—it's most alert and open to new information at this point.

Before you get out of bed, what do you think about? A dead-end job? A stressful relationship? A two-hour commute? An irritating manager or team leader? Suppose you made time to contemplate your upcoming day before you headed to the bathroom each morning. If there was a daily-life menu sitting on your lap, offering a variety of items that represented the type of day you could have, what would you see? Imagine that the menu had two pages, a page of entrees on the left and a page of entrees on the right. The page on the left represents entrees that could create an average day, and the page on the right represents awesome-day entrees.

Would your entrees be limited to just a few items? How much would they vary? Any specials? Would your subconscious tell you that you were out of awesome entrees? Knowingly or unknowingly, consciously or unconsciously, we choose entrees that represent the kind of day we're probably going to have. The disappointing reality is that most people go straight to the average side. And they order and eat the same stuff every day. Do you ever hear people, when asked how their day is going, say "Same old stuff"? Well, who's at fault?

The picture that comes to my mind in this case is of someone slowly rising up while sitting on the edge of the bed. He or she wipes the sleep and crust from their eyes and reaches down toward the floor. But rather than reaching for a comfortable pair of slippers, he or she hungrily reaches for their daily menu and opens it up to the AVERAGE choices. Thinking of speaking to an imaginary waiter, he or she says:

> I'll take the usual. For breakfast, I'd like to have one of those "Didn't hear my alarm and overslept" and a "Got stuck in traffic on the way to work." I'll take a side order of that "coffee stain on my tie" and give me a little helping of that "burn my forehead with my curling iron" and the "cafeteria closes as soon as I get there for my morning coffee." For lunch, I'll take a big helping of that "My boss is getting on my nerves." I wonder how that "My computer shut down" will taste? Anyway, I'll take a side of those "long, waste-of-time meetings where nothing gets accomplished." To drink, give me a "coffee burns my tongue." For dinner, you have to give me one of those "another late night at the office." For my two dinner sides, I'll take the "someone got the credit for one of my ideas" and the "no change for the tollbooth." Dessert? I'll take "a flat tire" and "a splitting headache."

The vision I see for someone choosing from the AWESOME entrees is significantly different:

> For breakfast, I'd like a slice of that "awesome morning workout," "a healthy, filling meal before I get into the office," and a "read at least 10 pages of my favorite book." I'll also take a side of "one of my all-time favorite songs is playing while I drive in." For lunch, I'd like to have a huge order of that "quick but meaningful in-and-out of the day care for toddler drop-offs or pick-ups" and one of those "the time just flies by as I zoom through my morning." I'd

also like a bowl of that "helping a co-worker through a difficult decision." For dinner, I'd like—but it must be well done—"an extremely productive day at the job I love." I'd also like, for one of my two sides, a "compliment from a co-worker on a job well done on one of my projects," and for the other side order, "a high-five from one of the facilities workers as I leave the building." For dessert, just give me a big helping of a "dinner with the people I love the most" and "a great night of rest."

We do have an enormous amount of power to determine what kind of day we're going to have.

But it doesn't stop there. When it comes to determining what clothes you're going to wear each day, do you choose clothes from the average side of the closet or the awesome side? The average side of the closet offers clothes that you just throw on. You don't feel particularly powerful or motivated in these clothes. Yes, they match and they fit (for the most part). But they're not the colors or the patterns or the cuts that make you feel or appear awesome and empowered.

The awesome side of the closet offers clothes that help you to feel powerful. They fit you extremely well, all over. The colors bring out your smile and your natural energy. They highlight or accent your best features. They're clothes that add an additional pep to your step, groove to your move, and glide to your stride. People usually comment on how good you look, and as a result your attitude and performance reflect how awesome you feel.

Unfortunately, many of us, because we're usually running late or we're tired, just reach into the average side of the closet and pull out the first thing we put our hands on. This is often the setup for an incredibly predictable, average day.

My friend Leann Bohn told me about a morning that recently tested her morning average-versus-awesome selection process.

"Last night my daughter, for some reason, couldn't go to sleep until after 11:00 p.m.," she began. "My son was awakened not much later by severe abdominal pains, which required a trip to the emergency room. Turned out that he had strep throat, not appendicitis. The fog was so thick on the drive back from the emergency room at 5:00 in the morning that I could hardly see. And on the way into work, the traffic was unusually heavy due to the torrential rainfall. At one point I had to slam on the brakes, causing the entire contents of my purse to spill out all over the floor of my car. When I finally got into work, I had so much to carry that my arms were full and I couldn't carry an umbrella. I arrived five minutes late, dripping wet. But all I kept saying to myself was, 'The AWESOME side of the menu, Leann, choose from the AWESOME side.' The rest of my day was pretty good after that. And as for the rain, I really didn't mind not having an umbrella. I'm beginning to appreciate just how great rain really feels."

Consider This: "In the end, it is important to remember that we cannot become what we need to be by remaining what we are." —Max de Pree

Each day we have the power to have an average day or an awesome day. What do you choose?

I'm reminded of a job I had that required a two-hour commute each way. During my second month with the company, there was a terrible ice storm. I left work early, thinking that my long commute might take twice as long as usual. I stopped to fill the tank with gas and get a few snacks in case I got stuck. Sure enough, as soon as I merged onto the main highway, I did get stuck.

AWESOME
ADVICE

I always affirm that the next day will be a great success. For instance, if I have a large class to facilitate, I affirm that the participants will be active learners, the information I provide will be useful to them, and I will do the best that I can. Throughout the day, I am consciously aware of my thoughts. Each time a worry pops into my head, I break it down to discover where it's coming from. Then I transform the worry into a more constructive and positive thought.

If I am facilitating the same material more than once in a day or a week, I make it less tedious by adding different activities for the participants. Negativity is virtually habitual in the corporate setting; therefore, I always include inspirational anecdotes and humor to lighten the mood of the classroom.

My motivation also comes from the photographs of smiling faces that are on my desk and cubicle walls. I have an extremely strong support system in my family and friends. Anytime I have a frustrating moment, I close my eyes and picture a loved one's smiling face, or I'll repeat to myself something happy that they said to me.

If I wake up in a sad mood, I bring a favorite CD with me to listen to in the car on my ride to work; I sing each song as loud as I can! In addition, whenever I feel restless, I direct my energy into creative endeavors: writing, singing, and painting.

—Assunta "Susie" F. Marino, Long Hill Township, NJ

So I listened to the radio, read the newspaper, and ate cherry Twizzlers while waiting for the traffic to move. I began to ration my Twizzlers when I realized I would be spending much of the night in my car on the highway with hundreds of other frustrated motorists. Impatient drivers skidded off the road into the embankment or unsuccessfully tried to maneuver across the embankment to exit the highway. "In a hurry to get stuck," I thought to myself as I continued my game plan of half a Twizzler every half hour.

I finally reached home at 3:30 a.m. My car died, and I ended up taking the rest of the week off to recover and to get my car repaired.

Thoughts of finding a new job danced through my head for a minute. No job is worth this everyday aggravation. But then I turned the pity party music off. Working for this company was the chance of a lifetime. I had connected with both my manager (Kathy Cook) and my vice president, and I was not going to let my long commute dampen my spirits.

So every morning before I headed to the car, rather than thinking about the stop-and-go parking lot traffic I was bound to face, I thought about what CDs I was going to listen to. My car also became a moving library for learning. I listened to motivational and educational tapes and did an awful lot of thinking, designing, and creating. I began to look forward to the commute, welcoming the opportunity to play personal, self-reflective catch-up. I spent the equivalent of one entire day in my car commuting each week.

In spite of my arduous drive, I still ordered AWESOME entrees from the daily-life menu. I was going to be all right. I was making a huge difference for my department and for the organization. I had developed an awesome reputation for supervisory and management development, and I loved my job. I even began doing my first in-house motivational presentations while there. What a training ground!

This enriching experience would soon come to an end, however. The commute and my newborn daughter, Daecia, ultimately caused my exodus. Because of my departure time in the morning and my return time in the evening, whenever I saw my little angel during the week she was asleep or waking me up at some ungodly hour in the morning full of tears. Moving was not an option because we had only been in our new "dream home" for less than a year. I would soon secure another job a lot closer to home. I had to spend more quality time with Daecia.

I think it's a given: For an awesome day, don't even consider the average entrees or the average side of the closet. Eat right! Dress right! And don't waver. Don't let other people's average mornings change your positive outlooks and perspectives. I once had a manager who would storm into the office some days. Nearly everyone else in the department would walk around on eggshells, not wanting to appear happy. Not me! I had already had an awesome morning before I got to the office.

I guess I'm greedy. I start thinking about my awesome entrees the night before as I lay in bed contemplating my tomorrow. This is another sensational time to do mental programming. Your conscious mind is most alert right before you call it a night.

In the process of consistently choosing to have awesome days, you will begin to see a shift in your thoughts, a shift in your behaviors and expectations, a shift in your life—an awesome shift! It becomes easier and easier! My college roommate and great friend Arvon Jordan puts it very clearly and very much into perspective. He always tells me that he made the move from average to awesome 20 years ago when he figured out that any day that he's blessed enough to wake up is an awesome, great day.

Moving from Average to Awesome

This chapter is not only about beginning your day on a positive note. It's also about the law of attraction and how significant your subconscious is in determining the results you achieve. This exercise will help you move from an average mindset to a more positive and powerful awesome way of living.

First, consider which statement describes how you prepare for the world each day:

- **Average:** You wake up on the wrong side of the bed, jump into the shower, jump into the car, and jump into another day of what LIFE has waiting for you.

- **Awesome:** You energetically begin each day by reading something spiritual, inspirational, motivational, or uplifting for 45 to 60 minutes; you review and create new goals for yourself; and you go for a walk or work out. You buy a mirror and hang it somewhere near the front door. Before leaving the house each day, you look at the mirror and say to yourself, "I'm awesome and I'm going to have an awesome day! Awesome starts now!" Then you confidently walk into your day—expecting to have an awesome one and not letting anyone kidnap your joy and enthusiasm.

Now, take some time and consider the questions below. Respond to the questions and be sure to explain your answers. Finally, rate yourself on your progress. If you are currently average, say so (A). If you feel you deserve an awesome rating, indicate that as well (AW). If you are neither average nor awesome but working toward being awesome, just write W.

Getting to Awesome

Key questions	Your response and explanation	Rating
What's your daily morning routine?		
Do you routinely have late nights that consist of working on the computer until the morning hours or drinking with friends and colleagues?		
Do you make excuses for your slow starts by saying "I'm not a morning person" or "I haven't had my first cup of coffee"?		

Rate your progress: average (A), awesome (AW), or working toward awesome (W).

Chapter 6

Fire Hard Kid!

> You can't teach people to be winners if they want to be whiners. Some things are innate. Simply do what you love and you will be positive. It's almost impossible not to be.
>
> —LISA MARZULLO, CHICAGO

Come on Shooter, fire hard, kid," Mr. Sam used to bark as he encouraged his pitcher to strike out the opposing team's batter. "Come on son, fire hard!"

Mr. Sam's bellowing shouts of "fire hard, kid" could probably be heard for miles, all the way from West Philly to North Philly. This powerful phrase became the team's rallying cry whenever we wanted our pitcher to throw strikes. You could hear it from the players on the field. You could hear it from the guys on the bench. You could even hear it from the parents and fans in the stands. "Fire hard, kid." It became one word, said very quickly and loudly: *"Firehardkid!"*

Mr. Sam's Jayhawks teams were an institution in West Philadelphia during the 1970s. You weren't considered a "real" ball player, we thought, until you wore a Jayhawks uniform. Hundreds of passersby would stop to watch our games.

Samuel Gallman was the Vince Lombardi, Bill Parcells, Pat Summit, and John Chaney of Little League baseball in West Philadelphia. The balding and graying, 50-something, six-foot-one husband and father was both a coach and an umpire. Mr. Sam, which is what everyone (adults and children) always called him, spent his summers teaching boys ages 10 to 18 about baseball, about life, and about self-respect. And respect is what he deserved and received from us. No one—not the opposing coaches, not the neighborhood tough guys, tough girls, or gang members, and certainly not the kids who played for or against him—ever disrespected the fiery coach.

But that didn't mean Mr. Sam's players were not targets for other abuse, fights, and threats. We played in many games where the neighborhood bullies, both in uniform and in street clothes, reminded us during the game that if we won the game they would certainly win the fight afterward. Imagine innocent 12-year-olds at bat while the neighborhood thugs yelled through the fence, "You get a hit, Shorty, and I'm going to jack you up!" "Your Mom is not going to be able to protect you. I'm going to kick your butt!" These were not just mind games. We often had to fight to get to our parents' cars and vans after the game. Mr. Sam was always in the thick of things, breaking up fights and doing his best to shield us from the hoodlums.

Nonetheless, with everything else Mr. Sam taught me, my most profound memory, the thing that still lingers in my mind, is the "Fire hard, kid." One play typified this spirit. The score was tied with two outs in the last inning and I was on second base. My teammate got a clutch base hit. As the outfielder made the throw into home, I rounded third base. Stopping at third wasn't even an option because I was firing hard. But the play wasn't even close: I was going to be out by a mile. The catcher, all 6-foot-2, 250-pounds-plus of him, caught the ball and waited for me to reach home plate. Sliding wasn't an option either, as I decided that the only way I was going to be safe would be to emerge the victor in a home plate collision with King Kong; I was 5-foot-7, 140-pounds of energy and/or stupidity. I crashed into the mountain of a teenager with everything I had. I slithered down his massive body like ice cream sliding down a cone on a humid day. I hurt all over! The catcher never budged, but my slight-yet-firing-hard impact knocked the ball from his glove. I was safe! We won the game! I was, indeed, firing hard!

As I moved from my Little League years through my teenage years to my adult years, I've always fired hard in whatever I did.

Merely showing up and only doing what I was asked was never enough. I always sat in the front of the class. I never believed in faking it until you make it. Pretending was for actors. We have to consistently and earnestly bring or give our absolute best, our "A game." And sometimes we have to weather the storm in the process. William Feather says that success seems to be largely a matter of hanging on after others have let go.

Consider This: "If you ask me what I have come to do in the world, . . . I will reply: 'I'm here to live my life out loud.'"
—Émile Zola

In my travels as a training consultant, I meet thousands of corporate, professional trainers. I usually share with them, early on, that I have good news and bad news. The good news is that there are thousands of good trainers out there. The bad news is that there are thousands of merely good trainers out there. I haven't come across nearly as many awesome trainers as I would have liked to, trainers who routinely "fire hard!"

Bob Pike, the highly respected and creative training techniques guru, once told me, after seeing me present, that I have more energy than any other trainer he's seen in his 40-plus years in the industry. This was after I had successfully auditioned for a spot on his coveted team of training professionals. My energy and drive come from my mother saying "There's always work to be done" and Mr. Sam yelling "Fire hard, kid!"

I've done all sorts of things in the classroom and in front of audiences that suggest I'm firing hard. I've lowered the classroom lights and performed funerals for the participant's "doubts" and "time-wasters," burying those toxic items (which they've written on sheets of paper and have committed to purging from their minds) in shoeboxes and then burning the remnants. From clapping hands, to stomping feet, to quickly changing seats, to the "sports clap," to the conga line, to the Soul Train review, to the triple kooshball review, participants *grow through* and not just *go through* my sessions.

I've gone from corporate to "cool" in front of participants' startled eyes when I discuss stereotyping and perceptions during diversity workshops. I change from wearing conservative Wall Street gear (that is, conservative eyeglasses, college ring, single-breasted gray suit, wing-tipped shoes, overly starched white shirt and power tie) to "yo baby yo baby yo" cool wear (dark sunglasses; earring; ripped T-shirt; pager; shorts; Malcolm X red, black, and green hat; and sneakers). I don't want to merely talk about stereotyping and perceptions, because that would not be firing hard or be memorable; I want you to actually feel and see it.

During my keynote motivational talks I'm in perpetual motion, providing a real-life visual aid for the points I drive home. I want participants to taste, feel, hear, smell, and see the learning moments and directional tips. I want them to inhale the inspiration and inhale my energy! To that end, I lug cumbersome props and visuals with me around the world. People always ask me why

I carry so much stuff. I just tell them that I'm firing hard. By the end of my sessions, participants are usually as exhausted as I am.

I often think about many of my colleagues who have secured mentors, attended professional development workshops, acquired various industry certifications, or taken lateral assignments to eventually move into the position they coveted. They were firing hard. I think of the many professionals I've met who have returned to school and to the workforce after rearing their children. They were firing hard, too.

When it comes to firing hard, Larry Boyd is a disciple. Much of that energy, Larry says, stems from his early childhood days in South Carolina. One particular school year, 1967–68, was crucial. The civil rights movement and the Vietnam war were in full force. The public schools in Larry's tiny hometown and other southern states were also being integrated. From grades one through three, Larry had attended all-black public schools. Just before he was about to start the fourth grade, his parents received a letter informing them that he would have to enroll in one of the integrated schools. Not wanting to leave his friends and start all over, he was initially extremely reluctant. He was also fearful, because he had seen marching and rioting on television and firsthand.

Larry wanted no part of going to a white school. He said it wasn't that he did not want to be around white students. He just did not want to be someplace where he did not feel he was wanted. His parents even tried enrolling him in his old school on the first day of class but were told that all his records had been sent to his new school. He had to attend school there.

His parents assured him that if he did his best, everything would be all right. Larry started firing hard! He took this new opportunity as a challenge to show his new white classmates, his teacher, and himself that he could excel academically and in any environment, despite the adversity. He was one of three black children in the class, and he soared. He soared through his remaining years at the school and on through high school, college, and the military. For the past 14-plus years, he has been a manager for a successful international nonprofit organization in Philadelphia that coaches, develops, tutors, and places talented minority college students in *Fortune* 25, 100, and 500 companies. He still maintains friendships with many of the students from his first integrated class. Moreover, a couple of years ago he took an extended leave of absence from the corporate world to return to the military to help his country in its war with Iraq.

There's an inner drive that moves us to move mountains. This drive moves us to study all night for a test after we haven't cracked the book for months. This drive moves us to spend all day cleaning up the house when we know guests are coming over that evening. This drive moved me to spend the Christmas and New Year's holidays hibernating in my office working on the revisions of this book when others were shopping, celebrating, vacationing, or getting their "eggnog on." In essence, WE FIRE HARD WHEN WE WANT TO FIRE HARD.

As it relates to anything you do in life, if you want to create the possibility for awesome results, you have to "fire hard, kid." If it means getting up super-early, if it means rewriting your class notes for the third time, if it means telling your friends that you will have to get together with them another time, if it means staying in on an absolutely gorgeous Saturday afternoon to finish studying or writing, if it means carrying additional props and supplies to make your presentations more memorable and outstanding, if it means doing tons of additional research before you interview for a job, and even if it means working for a boss or dealing with a professor or teacher who you *let* drive you batty, you still have to "fire hard, kid."

AWESOME
ADVICE

What makes me go from ordinary to extraordinary is the EXTRA. The extra effort and energy to raise the bar, to go 110 percent, I believe comes from attitude. I find that quotes help me be in the top 2 percent. So I encourage others to find those words that inspire you and reflect on the message daily and soon you will be performing at 110 percent. Some of my favorite quotes are

- "If you can't see the bright side, polish the dull side!"
- "Kind words make good echoes!"
- "We stand tallest when we stoop to help others!"
- "Setbacks pave the way for comebacks!"

—Doug McCallum, Lincoln, NE

Moving from Average to Awesome

This chapter is not only about giving your all in every aspect of your life. It's also about how the appropriate mindset can help you overcome huge challenges and obstacles. This exercise will help you move from an average mindset to a more positive and powerful awesome way of living.

First, consider which statement describes how you think about personal power:

- **Average:** You tend to settle for good results. You only "fire hard" during emergencies or when someone is watching.
- **Awesome:** You give your best effort regardless of the circumstances. You promise yourself, challenge yourself, and remind yourself to consistently "fire hard, kid!"

Now, take some time and consider the questions below. Respond to the questions and be sure to explain your answers. Finally, rate yourself on your progress. If you are currently average, say so (A). If you feel you deserve an awesome rating, indicate that as well (AW). If you are neither average nor awesome but working toward being awesome, just write W.

Getting to Awesome

Key questions	Your response and explanation	Rating
What motivates you to step up/ fire hard? Do you only step up/ fire hard when you have to?		
What types of challenges slow or derail you?		

How would others describe your personal power?		

Rate your progress: average (A), awesome (AW), or working toward awesome (W).

Chapter 7

Make Time, Not Excuses, for Your Loved Ones

> I keep a pretty good attitude about life by balancing out my personal life and my career. I keep burnout at a distance by engaging in the numerous activities outside of work that I enjoy.
>
> —TINA M. GREENE, BINGHAMTON, NY

If I had kept a running count, I would say that it happened 9 out of 10 times: Whenever I was working in my home office, my 6-year-old (at the time) daughter Daecia would ecstatically skip down the stairs and into the room and ask (as only a precious little daddy's girl could), "Daddy, can we play Reader Rabbit?" And 9 times out of 10, I would say, "Baby, Daddy is busy right now, we can play later." We both knew, however, that my "laters" were synonymous with "one day," "some day," "in 5 minutes," "eventually," and "when I get around to it." Dejected, she would slowly walk out, retreating upstairs to look for something else to do.

Over time, Daecia would come down to my office just to kiss me and tell me that she loved me. Her mini, non–Reader Rabbit-focused visits were obviously in response to my workaholic, insensitive regimen. One day, however, the gorgeous little kissing bandit came down to my office when I was in the midst of client calls, computer problems, and chaos. Before she could kiss and run, I grabbed her and said, "Let's play some Reader Rabbit." Her two-teeth-missing smile and boisterous "YES!" shone like a light turned on in the bedroom in the middle of the night. She plopped down on my lap in front and commandeered the mouse, and we had a Reader Rabbit great time. I had learned another valuable lesson.

We are awfully busy these days. We're too busy to take care of ourselves, and we're too busy to make time for the people who mean the most to us. This era of rapidly advancing technology has eliminated the B word (balance) from our vocabulary. Some of us feel guilty if we're not working. Where is the balance?

We take power naps. We multitask. We skip lunch. There are times when my flights land well after midnight. Arriving either at home or at a client site that late at night or that early in the morning is saddening. But arriving with hundreds of other workaholics is even more distressing. Sometimes I have to check my watch. The number of travelers in the airport would lead you to believe that it was midafternoon. The airports are packed with professionals too busy to enjoy life outside of their corporate responsibilities, BlackBerries, Palm Pilots, laptops, pagers, and cellphones. Sad, but true!

Daecia's desire to have more Reader Rabbit moments with her father was the slap in the face that I needed. I was practically living on the road; she helped me to realize that I was creating distance even when I was close—I behaved like I was still on the road when I was at home. My office became my sanctuary. With my desktop computer, fax machine, printer, television, stereo, telephones, window, bookshelf filled with resources, and refrigerator close by, I was set. I would only come out to the world to eat, go to the bathroom, and sleep. It was not uncommon for me to finally close down my office at 2:00 a.m.

Consider This: How are we going to savor our moments if we don't create them?

I had become a product of my insane society—always on the run, always in an airport, always rushing through conversations, always on the cellphone, always going to another meeting, always getting my morning workout in before 6:00 a.m., always wolfing down my food and always awakening before my wakeup call. I convinced myself that this was short-term pain for long-term gain. But who was I fooling? I had forgotten what my former manager, Kathy Cook, had told me—to work smarter, not always harder.

You receive myriad lessons in your lifetime, and many of the most powerful lessons originate from the hearts and minds of people who are too young to drink, drive, or stay up past 8:00 p.m. These little people love you in spite of your moments of anger, forgetfulness, morning breath, insensitivity, and poor time management.

Workaholics (a.k.a. work-and-family-balance dodgers)—you know who you are—repeat after me:

- I'm going to start making more time for the people I love.
- I'm going to start making more time for me.
- I'm going to slow down.
- I'm not going to make a "to-do" list every day.

AWESOME ADVICE

My attitude really went to a different level in May 1999 when my son, John Willis II, was born. He lived for 30 days but influenced more people in his 30 days than I have in my lifetime. He showed me that I have the chance to use his life as a way to influence people in my life. My desire is to influence children in this world as much as I can. I have a picture on my desk from Successories that says, "Priorities—A hundred years from now it will not matter what my bank account was, the sort of house I lived in, or the kind of car I drove . . . but the world may be different because I was important in the life of a child."

I have two children, Lauren, 6, and Matthew, 4, and my influence on them and any other child I encounter is what drives me to create a positive and outstanding environment around me.

—Jey Willis, Atlanta

- Sometimes, I'm going to wake up and just do nothing.
- I'm going to listen to more music and listen to the birds chirping.
- I'm going to stop reading the newspaper at the kitchen table during dinner.
- I'm going to read more positive, uplifting books.
- I'm going to go for more morning walks.
- I'm going to stop getting wakeup calls every day.
- I'm going to stop checking my stocks every day.
- I'm going to stop getting upset if I don't get a chance to check my emails every day.
- I'm going to stop gobbling down my meals.
- I'm going to start giving my undivided attention to the person I'm speaking to.
- I'm going to start playing more Reader Rabbit!

Life is gone too soon. Your life meter is always running. The quality times you spend with your loved ones are the coins that are needed to help keep your life meter running.

You're not going to believe this, but while I was writing this chapter, Daecia came into my office to play. What perfect timing! I did take a break, played some Reader Rabbit, savored the moment we just shared, and returned to writing *From Average to Awesome*—but not right away. We had dinner first.

How could I have been so negligent for so long? Daecia is my little angel. I wasn't blessed with her life until I was in my 30s. I had desperately wanted a child, and this was my way of showing my appreciation? Moreover, the relationship a little girl has with her Dad is precious and confirming.

Daecia still visits me in my office, although not as often, as she is approaching her teen years. It's usually to show me what she's wearing or to go online. Before going to bed every night, she finds me to do her kissing bandit thing. And a couple of her other favorite pastimes include shaving my bald head, rubbing my head at any given moment, and challenging me to a game of thumb war.

My Dad was not always there for me, so you would think I might have learned from that sobering reality. Shortly after our Reader Rabbit life lesson, I drove Daecia to school. I make it a habit to either drop her off or pick her up when I'm not collecting frequent flier miles flying to another client site. While we were riding, she totally caught me off guard by saying, "Daddy, tell me a story about what you learned from Grammy." I almost brought the car to a complete stop, floored by her poignant, thoughtful question. After I answered, fighting back one of the biggest smiles I've had since she was born, I winked at her.

As if she was on a roll, and I was a guest on her talk show, she fired Question #2, saying, "Daddy, tell me about what you and Uncle Rah Rah (my brother Rodney) used to do when you were small—what toys did you play with?" My GI Joe, Rock 'Em Sock 'Em Robots, and Hot Wheels answer cracked her up and was the sensational start to the day we both needed.

We can't get the time back. Turn in your 24/7-work-membership card. If more of us ripped those cards to shreds, we could eliminate such sardonic refrains as: "I owe, I owe, it's off to work I go" or "I work, I work, I'm becoming an insensitive jerk." Regain your balance. Create a place for rest and replenishment. You cannot be awesome if you're consistently working around the clock. Thanks for the reminder, Daecia!

Moving from Average to Awesome

This chapter is not only about working smarter and not harder. It's also about how important it is to have balance in your life to make quality time for your loved ones. This exercise will help you move from an average mindset to a more positive and powerful awesome way of living.

First, consider which statement describes how you think about the balance you have created in your life:

- **Average:** You fit everyone in around your schedule.
- **Awesome:** You consistently make quality time for yourself and for the people you love. You identify the things you do that take precious time away from you and your special people. You develop and follow through with a plan to remove those things from your schedule.

Now, take some time and consider the questions below. Respond to the questions and be sure to explain your answers. Finally, rate yourself on your progress. If you are currently average, say so (A). If you feel you deserve an awesome rating, indicate that as well (AW). If you are neither average nor awesome but working toward being awesome, just write W.

Getting to Awesome

Key questions	Your response and explanation	Rating
Do you keep promising to change your routine to create more balance but have not done so yet?		
Are you a workaholic?		
What are you going to do to overcome your BlackBerry and computer addiction?		

Rate your progress: average (A), awesome (AW), or working toward awesome (W).

Chapter 8

Do Your Homework, Then Ace Your Test

Set boundaries and live by them, but know when to be flexible and when to stand firm. Also, don't put yourself on a pedestal. Let someone else do that—it's safer that way.

—LAURA HUGHES, LEWISTON, ID

Have you ever bounced a check? No, not one where you made an honest checkbook mistake, inadvertently thinking you had enough money in your account to cover things. I'm referring to one of those occasions when you knew your account was on "E," but you nevertheless, boldly, aimlessly wrote the check anyway. Your hope and prayer was that miraculously, some way, somehow, you would be able to beg, borrow, or find the money to make the deposit into your account before the bank processed your rubbery piece of paper.

That's essentially what we do when we take on bad business. We knowingly exercise poor judgment, associating with individuals or taking on opportunities we know are not good for us, perhaps participating in something we know is going nowhere. Plain and simple: We know we shouldn't go there! It's tantamount to interviewing for a job with a company that has a huge "going out of business" sign in the front window.

A few years ago, while I still worked full time in the corporate world, I occasionally took a personal day off from work to do a consulting, training, or speaking job. These jobs provided valuable entrepreneurial experience. Not only did these experiences give me a glimpse into what owning my own business would be like, they also served up opportunities to work with companies that viewed me as the hired gun, the outside consultant.

I stumbled onto one client, in particular, whom other consultants in the industry—as well as other employees in the client's company—insisted I should avoid.

People consistently told me that there was one department in the company that was "bad business." My colleagues said that taking on work for this company was OK, but taking on work for one particular senior leader was akin to bullfighting with a Kleenex, blindfolded. They said that this powerful, demanding, and extremely crass senior leader ran an extremely tight, autocratic ship. The word on the street was that the department was "Stepfordish."

This news caused me to hesitate for a day, reevaluating my former manager's warning about taking on bad business, but I moved forward anyway. Besides, the person who called with the opportunity was following up on a family member's referral. Her relative had seen me facilitate a similar presentation when she and I both worked for the same firm. I decided to make my decision after the caller and I discussed the opportunity over lunch.

During lunch, she said that her relative had blurted out over the phone, "You have to get him—he's outstanding!" Moreover, my future client was an extremely warm and caring person. She created an awesome vision for me for future work with the company. I was salivating over the prospect of repeat business, especially because I was exploring starting my own business. This would be my first extended client opportunity!

We connected immediately. I was going in!

I presented a seamless case to myself. My closing argument was phenomenal. I convinced myself that my style was different from the consultants who had gone into this snake pit before me. My style was more energizing, more participant-driven, I reasoned. Based on the many successes I'd had with my full-time employers, I believed that I was ready for a challenging client—a stretch assignment. This would be another opportunity to test my skill set and would certainly help once I finally went out on my own.

The contract was for two engagements: one was a lunchtime train-the-trainer session for their corporate trainers; the other, a motivational keynote for the entire "risky business" department. I saw opportunity, not suicide. I envisioned high-fives, not finger pointing. This was a chance to put a major *Fortune* 100 company at the top of my referral list, not at the back of my mind.

As I'd hoped, the first session rocked! Kudos, smiles, plaudits, and handshakes were plentiful. I felt relieved and sensational. I did it! Conversations and plans for my returning on a monthly basis were immediately under way. What were my colleagues talking about, I thought? It was just a matter of truly believing in oneself.

Round two was different. Ding! Ding!

I facilitated the 60-minute keynote, motivational presentation for the "risky business" department. Nonstop, I energetically and passionately shared encouraging words of hope, action, and direction. I got the participants involved, inspired, clapping their hands and laughing. After the final "Thank you," they gave me a standing ovation. I did it . . . I did it . . . I did it again, I thought. I was glad I took the risk. Many motivational sayings were dancing in my mind. "Obstacles are what you see when you take your eyes off of your goals." "No one can make you feel inferior without your consent." "Only those who risk going too far will ever know how far they can go." My colleagues were mistaken again.

One of the other client managers even walked me around the room, introducing me to several of the managers who had lingered around the lunch spread. I was taking my Cal Ripken victory lap and feeling the thrill of victory.

Little did I know how soon my exultation would be squelched by the agony of defeat.

I asked one of the pretzel-munching managers what he thought about the presentation. He hesitated, then said, "Jim, I thought it was great. Quite frankly though, it doesn't make any difference what I or anyone else thinks, it's what Hal Stern (the senior leader) thinks that matters."

I was stunned, wondering if the standing ovation I had received minutes earlier was live or Memorex. He continued, "Look outside, it's sunny right? If Mr. Stern said that it was snowing right now, everyone else in the department would rush to leave the office immediately to avoid the traffic jams caused by the inclement weather. Sounds strange, doesn't it? But that's the way things are around here." He said to wait a few days. The verdict would soon be in.

Upon my return to my office later that afternoon, I was welcomed by a voicemail message from the client manager whom I had taken to lunch. She was calling to talk about the session. Bubbling with enthusiasm, she said that in her opinion, I was incredible! She said the session was just what they wanted and that I had really delivered. Whew, I was relieved!

The next day, my check bounced.

When I called back to get additional feedback, my calls were not returned. I then received another call from the same client manager who had left the "vote of confidence" voicemail. She reminded me that I had left some of my props in their conference room and that I should come in to pick them up. I immediately heard the change in her voice—from cheerleader to the foreman of the jury. "What was that about?" I asked myself.

The overdraft notice and the verdict had come in at the same time.

She said that Mr. Stern had loathed the presentation. He had several peculiar, choice words that I believed were targeted at me both personally and professionally—words that I had heard before to describe assertive, confident, black men. He said that I was pompous, insensitive, arrogant, and self-centered. "Am I missing something?" I thought. "What do these adjectives have to do with the presentation? Didn't I receive a standing ovation?"

He went on to say that I was disrespectful for not asking for his permission to use his name in one of my examples. Huh?!?!?! Was he serious? Did he think I was one of his children? In using his name, I said something like, "If I was Mr. Stern, I would want all of my employees to come to work fired up every day, prepared to make an incredible contribution to the organization."

In addition, he said that if I had known more about the organization's "family" culture, I would not have used the word "ass" in another example. He *was* right with that one. He concluded his feedback with a clear, "stern" insistence that I never use his organization as a recommendation or referral. To say I was incensed would belabor the obvious. It's like saying Jamie Foxx deserved the Oscar for *Ray*, that Celine Dion can sing, that Maya Angelou writes beautiful poetry, or that Jackie Chan does a lot of stunts. Duh!

To further complicate matters, my two other client managers (who were both black) refused to return my calls. Communicating strictly through the first manager (also black), they told her to inform me that my presentation had made things miserable for them in the office because they were responsible for my being there, and that I would probably be the last black consultant to do work there. You've got to be kidding, I thought. Did the hands of time just turn back 75 years?

Mr. Stern (who was white) had called them all into his office and questioned their judgment for bringing me in. He was going to reconsider their upcoming promotions, and they would have to run future consultant choices by him. I eventually, briefly, spoke with one of the managers who had been avoiding my calls. He began our discussion in a scolding manner saying, "Didn't I tell you not to . . ."

This experience was beginning to smell awfully foul. The entire ordeal had "bad check" written all over it.

I was having a nightmare, but I had deposited the bad check. I let that incident rock my desire to continue motivational speaking. I had a 2,880-minute pity party. I temporarily forgot that someone's opinion of you does not have to become your reality. Nonetheless, within a couple of days, I got really mad, got sad, got better, and then got busy.

I deeply pondered Mr. Stern's targeted feedback. Some of it, I had to admit, was accurate, but most of it felt personal. I thought about the two client managers who did a complete about-face, initially showering me with praise, then with silence. I wondered what their jobs would be like going forward and how it must be to work in that kind of "camouflaged" wholesome, yet clearly hostile, environment. Although I was livid over what had happened, in a way I felt sorry for them.

As their consultant, I was not going to pay that same price to assimilate. That would have been killing my soul, my spirit, my energy, me. I was not willing to give up my values, my beliefs, and myself to become the type of speaker Mr. Stern would appreciate. That price was too high! But it was a price, I sensed, that they were paying every day. Alice Walker's poem resonated in my mind:

No man is your friend who demands your silence, or denies your right to grow.

Were my two presentations that vastly different? I also considered the frigid reception I received from the others in the department when I returned to retrieve my supplies. From hero to zero, champ to chump in less than a week. Most important, however, I thought about the colleagues who had warned me that this opportunity was bad business, and not to deposit the bad check.

I called Kathy Cook and explained what had happened. Rather than spending time telling me "I told you so," she asked me what I had learned from this experience. My answer was extremely heartfelt. I told her that I couldn't help but think that race had played a role in what happened. The senior leader's feedback was too personal. If his feedback had been more pointed toward my behavior, my information, my materials and ideas, and not my character, I would have felt differently. I just felt weird about the whole experience. My gut suggested that he was more than just a dissatisfied customer.

Kathy listened intently because she knew I seldom used race to substantiate my corporate misfortunes. People of color often feel race is the only reason for corporate crashes. Race is sometimes the reason, but it's not the only possible reason. People of color, at times, rush to the race case rather than rushing to exploration, making sincere efforts to uncover what else could be causing their dilemma. But, after exploring every conceivable option imaginable, I decided that race was my final answer. It was my story, and I was sticking to it.

I told Kathy that the entire experience made me feel sick. I believed Mr. Stern was holding me, for some reason, to a different standard. He had shut down the entire system. They gave me a standing ovation. In no corporate culture would they do that just to be polite.

AWESOME ADVICE

Throughout my career, I've had a number of opportunities to manage people and have found myself making some consistent mistakes. I have selected individuals without enough objectivity and rigor. Several years ago, I was involved in filling a key position in my company and was under pressure to do it quickly. We were committed to finding a diverse pool of candidates although, because of the assignment and the war for talent, we knew it would be difficult. When an African American female candidate was presented to us by the search firm, we were so thrilled that we didn't do the usual due diligence to ensure that this would be the right hire for us. We were too emotionally invested—and ended up with an individual who was a complete mismatch with our company culture and with a lot of heartache on both sides of the process.

I have given underperformers too much rope and then personally taken up the slack. I consider myself a person who possesses a fair bit of emotional intelligence, with the ability to size up people well. Having said that, I have on more than one occasion given people the benefit of the doubt way beyond what was reasonable.

In one particular case, I hired a well-regarded consultant for a significant fee. He was extremely effective in his interactions with the senior management team but gave little attention to the details and follow-up work that were also part of our agreement. However, given his popularity within the company, I resisted confronting him until I realized that I was overfunctioning and doing 50 percent of what I had hired him to do. Eventually I had to sever the relationship, but I should have done it much sooner.

—Ann Perington, Orange, CA

I told her how astonished I was by the behavior of the other blacks who had worked with me on the project. They certainly were not going to jeopardize their jobs (why should it have to come to that?) for my sake.

I even owned my part of the mess. I could have said rear end instead of "ass." But I went from standing ovation to standing in the cold. It was like a punch in the gut. I did not think my sentence was just.

Kathy said that one of the reasons I did so well with my other full-time employers was that my white colleagues had the opportunity to get to know me, to trust and respect me, to see me in action, time and time again. "By getting to know you, they got a chance to get to know your character and find out what you were all about," she continued. "Owning your own business, especially one that involves speaking and consulting, sometimes means being flexible, altering your style when you have to, to suit the client's needs. But you have to be true to yourself. Still, Jim, it was bad business. Everyone told you not to go in there! Some lessons are painful, aren't they?" We laughed. But deep inside, I was still reeling.

Let me share with you the "after-Kathy" quiet conversation I had with myself, because although this was a bad-check-depositing experience, it felt like a lot more:

> Is this stuff (that is, prejudice) ever going to stop? I don't let everything get to me—I'm not supersensitive—but some things leave deep wounds. This was just plain stupid! Just when I'd thought I had built an internal force field to repel ignorant, prejudicial treatment, I was done in again. All my other race-related experiences, I thought, were the dress rehearsals. I thought I had moved to a place where sticks and stones could break my bones but racial names and games could never hurt me. I've had 13 years of corporate experience and 36 years (at that point) of living. I

was about to start my own business. And what about all of my years as a diversity consultant? Nothing has ever affected me as strongly as this episode. One powerful, "stern," man reminded me that life's not fair. But I'll get through it. I have to! There is a blessin' in every lesson.

Sometimes rose-colored glasses are difficult to remove. Nevertheless, you've got to "see the forest for the trees," "wake up and smell the coffee," and "don't take on bad business." Knowingly exercising poor judgment comes back to bite you every time.

Consider This: "It's what you learn after you know everything that counts."
—John Wooden

Resist those urges (you know what urges I'm talking about). Avoid thinking that your "fate credit card" will never max out. Know that some situations are totally out of your control. You don't always have to be a Braveheart or Wonder Woman. Start managing your life's checkbook better! Stop depositing bad checks!

Moving from Average to Awesome

This chapter is not only about being more discerning. It's also about how you should learn from past foibles and know what your blind spots are. This exercise will help you move from an average mindset to a more positive and powerful awesome way of living.

First, consider which statement describes how you think about taking on new opportunities:

- **Average:** You jump into the fray without doing your homework, relying solely on your instincts and talents.

- **Awesome:** You use sound judgment. You consider the wisdom of the people you believe in and do not ignore the obvious. You develop a keen sense of what's right and what's wrong. You remember that sometimes no matter how promising an opportunity may seem, it's not for you.

Now, take some time and consider the questions below. Respond to the questions and be sure to explain your answers. Finally, rate yourself on your progress. If you are currently average, say so (A). If you feel you deserve an awesome rating, indicate that as well (AW). If you are neither average nor awesome but working toward being awesome, just write W.

Getting to Awesome

Key questions	Your response and explanation	Rating
What drives the decisions you make?		
Are you sometimes accused of ignoring the obvious?		
Do you consistently find yourself in situations you can't get out of? Do you find yourself committing the same mistakes, then not taking responsibility?		

Rate your progress: average (A), awesome (AW), or working toward awesome (W).

Chapter 9

Stop Taking Life So Seriously

> It's simple: I love, love, love, love feeling good! When I smile and laugh, I come alive. And when I'm alive, everyone around me comes alive and then I really feel good.
>
> —AILEEN DIZON, SACRAMENTO

The next time you're walking around in a train station or airport, standing on a street corner, waiting for a bus, or sitting at a traffic light, peer around slowly, security-camera style. Do some people watching. Look at their facial expressions, nonverbal communications, and body language. Take note of the number of people you see smiling and those who look somber. Count the smiles. Total the frowns. The number of depressed-looking people will amaze you. It's frightening.

Just by looking around for that very, very brief moment, you'll notice this eerie trend of negativity. I'm not sure if it's because of the anxiety-filled times we live in or the fact that myriad people tend to see the glass as half empty, but many—if not most—of the people you'll spot will appear to be in a funky mood, annoyed, frustrated, late for something, mad at the world, or wearing tight shoes that rub their corns the wrong way. Look around, and you'll see a great deal of defeat, depression, and despair.

Why are so many of us in such a morbid state? People make it easy for me to develop anecdotes, metaphors, and other material for my motivational keynotes. All I have to do is keep my eyes open and pay attention to what's going on around me.

I read a health and wellness periodical last year in which an article suggested that, on average, children laugh approximately 400 times a day. Adults, on the other hand, laugh approximately 15 times a day. Of course children don't have the same mammoth worries that we do. Other than during meals, their plates are never full. Their cars never break down. They don't have bad backs. They don't have to pay taxes. They don't have bills. They're not in sorry relationships. They don't get laid off, merged, or acquired. They don't have employees who routinely call in sick at the 11th hour. No one is providing them with a steady diet of deplorable customer service. These, however, are just excuses adults make for their unhappiness. Stop! I once read that a happy and successful person is someone who can build a firm foundation with the bricks that others throw at him or her.

Smiling and laughing are such leveling tools. Smiles and laughter are healthy, spontaneous expressions of life. Smiles really put people at ease. And the more you smile, the easier it becomes. I love to laugh. I just love feeling good—not taking this world or myself so seriously.

In my field of work, there are plenty of opportunities for me to take myself too seriously. Presenters, consultants, speakers, and trainers carry their egos with them along with their briefcases, driver's licenses, evaluation forms, and speech notes. But because we are so exposed, presenting in front of audiences of all sizes, we leave ourselves open for mistakes. We're very vulnerable. During presentations we trip, drop things, lose track of our thoughts, and don't always know when our opened button or low zipper is providing a view into a part of our world that audience members shouldn't be seeing. Smiling, laughing, and not taking those mishaps too seriously get me through those times.

I remember when a colleague forgot to take off his microphone during a session break. After we dismissed the group to their pagers, Palm Pilots, and cellphones, he hurried to the bathroom, unfortunately forgetting to turn off his microphone in his haste. Those who stayed in the classroom during the break were treated to special bathroom sound effects. We heard it all, including the flush. Upon his return to the room, we all enjoyed a hearty laugh.

I also remember when another co-trainer, Lydia, inadvertently lifted her dress in front of the class. One of the participants had said something that was pretty funny, and Lydia bent over laughing. While bending over, she lowered her leader's guide to her knees, touching the bottom of her dress. When she raised the guide to resume training, she inadvertently grabbed the bottom of her dress, bringing it up above her waist along with her leader's guide. Her slip saved her from an even more embarrassing moment. The other comical part about this was that she did not immediately realize what she had done. She kept training. Once we finally let her in on our little secret, she blushed, turning a shade very close to burgundy, and responded, "That's why my mother always told me to wear clean underwear." We all laughed.

I learned many years ago that smiling could also be the serum for other ills. My Mom told me some time ago to get into the habit of smiling, especially for identification photos. I believed then that Mom's main objective was to help others perceive me favorably—to help them feel comfortable with me. I would later find out that she had other reasons.

Yes, it was yet another one of her savvy lessons—to teach me to protect myself (you get more bees with honey) by flashing my 32 pearly white teeth and two deep dimples. In any identification photo I've ever taken, I have always had a big, someone's-tickling-my-feet smile. I believe those photos have had a positive impact on people and have erased some stereotypical thinking.

Consider This: "We would worry less about what others think of us if we realized how seldom they do."
—Ethel Barrett

I meet many people during my workshops and speaking sessions. I'm still amazed at the overwhelming level of seriousness I encounter at the beginning of these sessions. The typical facilitator begins the session by saying good morning. The participants' customary reply is barely audible. Having mastered the routine, the facilitator repeats herself by saying good morning again. The participants, realizing they'd sounded like fans watching a golfer attempt a match-clinching, eight-foot putt at the Masters, respond by saying good morning more loudly.

Sometimes I wonder if participants see me more as a proctor for an SAT exam than as a management development consultant and motivational speaker. I show up to build them up, not tear them down. My goal is always the same: to help them personally and professionally.

I understand that there is a certain level of personal and professional tension before any workshop or event. The typical participant enters the workshop thinking, "Will I ask a stupid question?" "Will I learn what's being taught?" "Will I connect with the people at my table?" "Is this going to be worth it?" Or:

"Why did my manager make me come here?" "I hope they finish early!" "I wonder if they're serving lunch?"

As a presenter, one of my initial goals is to make that tension vanish immediately. I want to break into whatever is preoccupying the participants. Many times, before the session gets started, I roam the room introducing myself. Sometimes I ask the participants to shake hands with, high-five, or hug at least 10 people they haven't yet met. That really helps them break through their pre-session comas. And if it is a group where everyone knows each other, the instructions vary just slightly: to shake hand with, high-five, or hug at least 10 people not sitting near you. I think it's strategic and responsible to begin your sessions before you start your sessions. The participants get so fired up and excited that it makes it extremely easy for me to then open with a bang.

I wear a smile every day. Laughter is one of the greatest preventive medicines. Laughter helps you feel better. Laughter moves all the muscles in your body. When you laugh, you create a positive expectation toward life. You have better thoughts, which lead to better actions, better behavior, and better results. And it's contagious.

Here's a case in point. Ten weeks away from home for basic training in pharmaceutical sales (including 24 exams) stood between Carolyn Moss and her hitting the field as a sales representative. But the instructor, Kathleen, was (according to Carolyn) the epitome of enthusiasm and dedication.

Although Kathleen was five months pregnant, she still worked the group until 1:00 a.m., making sure everyone felt comfortable with the material and overall job expectations. "Jim, there had to be times when she was frustrated, annoyed, and lacking motivation, but you would have never known it," Carolyn said. "Swollen ankles and all! I've never felt more welcomed than when I joined the company. When my day turns blue, I think of Kathleen. Now,

AWESOME ADVICE

I am a child of the North and, although I have traveled and lived around the world, I have never forgotten the happy, spirited, positive views of my childhood.

I come from a place where the sun follows the pattern of rest and run. This creates a sustaining abundance of light to fuel the harvest and the soul and the darkness that creates a balance of rest and reflection. This helps to spawn new possibilities as the green and pink aurora borealis dances in waves across the night sky's black stage. I come from a place where, for thousands of years before me, people developed personal mastery of their skills and learned to appreciate the harshness without which the beauty could not exist, where personal responsibility for self and others is entwined in the thread of survival.

I come from a place where each day is a new canvas to be painted, and I am compelled to paint.

I come from a place that reminds me that every person I meet will bring a gift of the community thread. I look for that gift, and I look for opportunities to affirm the gift each person brings.

I come from an awesome place, and it compels me every day to look with awe and appreciation at the goodness in people, places, circumstances, and creation. It is this childhood sense of awe that now has language, and it has been translated into three simple things: appreciation, affirmation, and abundance. Alaska lives in me, and that is what keeps me awesome and what keeps me smiling.

—Catherine Woods, Union, NJ

as a trainer, I hope to bring to the new trainees the same joy that she brought to my group. Her smile never went away!"

Start laughing right now, and I guarantee that the people around you will start laughing too. Go ahead, laugh. See, I told you.

I laugh in my sessions and I laugh in my car. I laugh all the time and it feels awesome. The people around me are definitely affected. Once you start laughing and smiling more, you'll see what I'm talking about. People will start hanging around you because they'll want some of what they think you have.

Take a cue from the toddlers of this world. Their anthem, with thanks to Bobby McFerrin, is "Don't worry, be happy!" It's all relative. In his book *The Prophet*, Kahlil Gibran says that "the same things that bring you sorrow bring you joy." Stop appearing so serious. Watch the children. Watch the laughter. Watch the fun. Watch out, it's contagious. Say cheese! It's easy and it works! It helps you to move to awesome!

Moving from Average to Awesome

This chapter is not only about taking life too seriously. It's also about how contagious your smile and positive energy can be. This exercise will help you move from an average mindset to a more positive and powerful awesome way of living.

First, consider which statement describes how you think about your spirit and countenance:

- **Average:** You look serious, only occasionally mustering up a smile. You only laugh when you watch funny movies, television shows, or comedians.
- **Awesome:** You don't take life so seriously. You enjoy the people and things around you. You smile and laugh just because you

can. You don't let every minuscule thing set you off. You take more deep breaths or just start to laugh when you feel you're about to explode with anger.

Now, take some time and consider the questions below. Respond to the questions and be sure to explain your answers. Finally, rate yourself on your progress. If you are currently average, say so (A). If you feel you deserve an awesome rating, indicate that as well (AW). If you are neither average nor awesome but working toward being awesome, just write W.

Getting to Awesome

Key questions	Your response and explanation	Rating
Are you often accused of being too serious?		
How would you and others describe your approachability?		
Do people easily connect with you?		

Rate your progress: average (A), awesome (AW), or working toward awesome (W).

Chapter 10

Become the CEO of *You*

> I live each day choosing to be who I am. For my life, the real meaning and sense of fulfillment come *not* from what I choose to do but from whom I choose to be. I don't let other things or other people define me. I look for ways to connect with people in a way that alters the air around us.
>
> —LISA DOMMER, COLUMBUS

I headed to David Kelliher's house to discuss my promotional video and website. My brother introduced me to Dave a couple of years ago, and we connected immediately. He has been my video and website manager ever since. Maybe it was the former jock thing (Dave played football for East Stroudsburg University) or the fact that we both have an amazing entrepreneurial spirit, having left our former employers to run our own businesses. We had already worked on several projects together, and we were meeting to strategize about the upcoming year.

I pulled into Dave's quiet, suburban driveway, unaware of the valuable life lesson I was going to take home with me along with all my meeting notes. Life lessons are like relationships—they find you when you're not looking for them.

My 100-percent-all-American friend, as he likes to refer to himself, is the epitome of thoroughness, organization, and effective feedback. Dave met me at the door and we went straight upstairs to his office to work. After our long but extremely productive meeting, I packed my materials, walked down the steps, and headed out the front door. As I walked toward my SUV, Dave caught me off guard by asking, "What are you, a walking billboard for the NFL?" Startled, I said, "What are you talking about?" Before Dave could reply, I looked down at what I was wearing, and then realized what was up. I was wearing a replica Tampa Bay Buccaneers jersey with Warrick Dunn's name and number (28) and a Minnesota Vikings cap. All I needed was a pair of Philadelphia Eagles sweatpants and Dave would have been perfect.

But those were my walking clothes, my relaxing, "take it easy" gear. I dressed that morning thinking about comfort, not that I was going to look like an *ESPN Primetime* groupie. The thought that I resembled a page from a professional football team catalog never crossed my mind when I took that last "vanity" look in the mirror before leaving the house.

Becoming defensive, I said, "Dave, I have a few jerseys that I sometimes wear and I collect hats wherever I go—this just happened to be the one I grabbed off of the shelf this morning." He laughed. "You're in denial, Jim. Do they pay you to do all this marketing for them? And Warrick Dunn must be pretty special to you for you to want to walk around all day with his name on your back." That one stung!

"Dave is on to something," I thought. As if he were the professor and I were his student, I began to share my takeaways from his revelation. "You're right man, so many of us walk around wearing team jerseys with athletes' names on the back," I began, "and on the surface, you know, there doesn't appear to be anything wrong with that. But the sports stars don't know us, and probably couldn't care less. I wonder what would happen if we wore more clothes that said who we are and what we are about."

"That's especially true for you, Jim," Dave said. "Since you have your own business, you should be wearing JIMPACT Enterprises stuff." Again, Dave's comment landed on GO.

I finished putting my meeting materials into my SUV, shook Dave's hand, put the key in the ignition, and rolled the window down. "See you later, Warrick," Dave joked. "Dave, I got it, I got it," I replied with a laugh.

I had had another educational moment. I drove away with plenty on my mind and another chapter for the book and for my life. Thanks to Dave, I had yet another impromptu conversation with myself as I headed down the street, back home to New Jersey.

My "Jim talking to Jim" conversation sounded like this: "Jim, face it, you're a sports nut. Always have been. Sports have been a part of your life since you and Rodney used to turn your dining room into a basketball court. Remember the electric football marathons? How about playing touch football in the street? Drove your neighbors crazy, but that didn't stop you from diving on parked cars to catch the ball.

"You played half-ball, whiffleball, dodge ball, baseball, basketball, football, step ball, wall ball—man you used to just play ball! Remember when you used to sit on the front step or lie in the bed listening to Phillies games on the radio, keeping the scorebook? Hey, what about when you were in college sitting through a boring lecture? You used to list the numbers 1 to 99 on a sheet of paper and write the name of an active sports star that wore that number. Number 44 was always Reggie Jackson. Number 6 was Dr. J. Now you collect team hats and you also have several team replica jerseys that you like wearing. Your favorites are your Houston Oilers Warren Moon jersey; your Wes Hopkins and

Donovan McNabb Philadelphia Eagles jerseys; your Randy Moss Minnesota Vikings jersey; your Philadelphia Flyers Eric Lindros jersey; and your New York Yankees shirt. You even have your own 1979–82 Widener University and 1979 *Philadelphia Daily News* City football all-star game jerseys. Maybe Dave was playing with your head. Maybe you're blowing this thing way out of proportion."

But then another thought bungee-jumped into my head. It ended my inner turmoil.

During business trips, I often get asked if I'm a fan of the team whose jersey or hat I'm wearing. My apparel has become a conversation starter. I never considered the significance of that before. Oh, wait. . . . Yes, I did. During my senior year at Widener University, I used to wear prescription-less glasses and a blazer or preppy sweater and at times carry a briefcase. I wanted the faculty, administration, and student body to see me as a student first and football player second.

So when business travelers ask me if that is my favorite team, I just say no, and that I collect hats and this just happens to be the one I chose to wear. Sometimes I get into lengthy sports conversations because of the hat I'm wearing. Because I'm on the road so frequently, I meet tons of people in airports, in restaurants, on planes, and while waiting for taxis. What if they were asking about JIMPACT Enterprises, my interests, and me rather than if I was a Philadelphia Flyers fan when I wore my number 88 Lindros jersey?

I'm not Tiger Woods. I don't want to be like Mike. I don't eat Chunky Soup because Donovan McNabb, his mother, and the Eagles do. Yao Ming, Venus and Serena, Allen Iverson, Kevin Garnett, Derek Jeter, Roger Federer, Steve Nash, and Peyton Manning are merely athletes that I root for. And don't be mistaken, I cheer as loudly as the most diehard fan. But that's it. When we wear their names on our backs, our admiration soars to another,

AWESOME
ADVICE

People, my students, always knew what I was about. I've worn it on my sleeve forever. I still wear it today. I'm so predictable! I do things my way. Regardless of what's happening, I'm always on the positive side. I always walk away from negativity. I stay away from things that don't have a positive impact on my thinking. People know I am who I am.

—Dr. Frank "Tick" Coleman, Philadelphia, age 93, who got his driver's license in 2001 at the age of 90 and had his left leg amputated that same year frightening level. I can still hear Dave's words, "I never see them wearing your name on their backs."

You may be thinking that I'm exaggerating this point. But consider this: If we put as much time, focus, and effort into developing and sharpening our skills as we do acquiring and wearing the latest team jersey, how much better would our professional realities be? Wearing your favorite team's jersey at the game is one thing—and wearing their hat and shirt during a championship run is another—but every day, every weekend, every night to bed? Come on!

It gets worse! Brand names, designer jeans, "Air-this," "LeBron-that," and company logos are ubiquitous. Everything has a corporate logo slapped on it. You have the Staples Center, the Fleet Center, the Wachovia Center, Heinz Field, Minute Maid Park, Citizen's Bank Park, and Coors Field. What ever happened to the Boston Garden, the Astrodome, Mile High, and Three Rivers Stadium? How long will it be before we say goodbye to Yankee Stadium, Wrigley Field, Fenway Park, and Madison Square Garden? The Tweeter Center near Boston used to be called the Great Woods Center for the Performing Arts. I couldn't help but snicker when the former undisputed middleweight boxing champion Bernard Hopkins had the name and telephone number of a gambling establishment painted on his back during a championship fight.

We're becoming all the "stuff" that promotes superstars and the corporate world yet drains our pockets and our focus. We work endless hours and save money for the privilege of promoting someone else. Consider the growing obsession with sports stars, entertainers, and movie stars and the paraphernalia that goes along with it (T-shirts, throwback jerseys, banners, posters, magazines, and more). And when wearing their names on our backs or on our feet is not enough, we dress just like them. Some misguided people now get plastic surgery to look more like their favorite celebrities. Think of all the young girls dressing "babe-aliciously" to emulate Beyoncé, the Pussycat Dolls, Fergie, Mary J. Blige, Pink, and Christina Aguilera and all the young boys dressing like Jay-Z, Eminem, Nelly, Justin Timberlake, Usher, 50 Cent, and Diddy and other rap stars, all of whom present grossly distorted images of the masculinity and femininity to which kids aspire. Quite an irony that in a country that claims to value the individual, we follow the fads with a mind-numbing conformity. We lose ourselves in the process. And if we're not dressing like them, we're buying clothes from their clothing line.

Consider This: "Know thyself and become who you are." —Socrates

Many of us could spend more time appreciating and loving ourselves—even marketing our own talents and abilities. Could doing something that appears so insignificant on the surface (that is, limiting the team, designer, and brand name apparel you routinely wear) begin to change what's in your head? I think so!

Invest in yourself! Literally or figuratively invest in YOUR team. Buy a jersey with your name on it. Stay grounded. Stay centered. Wear a jersey that allows you to grow, to blossom, and to realize your goals. Wear a jersey that creates opportunities for you to share your talents—one that draws people to you because of who you are and not because you root for a particular team. As the Indian sage Muktananda said, "Go everywhere, do everything, meet everyone, love everyone, but never forget to love yourself."

Moving from Average to Awesome

This chapter is not only about self-discovery and self-appreciation. It's also about how having the courage, wherewithal, and savvy to share your individuality. This exercise will help you move from an average mindset to a more positive and powerful awesome way of living.

First, consider which statement describes how you think about self-development and self-esteem:

- **Average:** You only occasionally read a self-development book or watch a movie, and then you haltingly vow to make changes when you can fit them into your schedule.
- **Awesome:** You spend considerable time developing yourself and doing those things that stimulate others to want to connect with you for yourself—not because of your team jersey or designer outfits. You wear team jerseys only when rooting your team on to victory.

Now, take some time and consider the questions below. Respond to the questions and be sure to explain your answers. Finally, rate yourself on your progress. If you are currently average, say so (A). If you feel you deserve an awesome rating, indicate that as well (AW). If you are neither average nor awesome but working toward being awesome, just write W.

Getting to Awesome

Key questions	Your response and explanation	Rating
Do you routinely overconcern yourself with how others feel about you?		

What do you do to invest in yourself?		
Are you willing to stand for your principles and beliefs regardless of who is suggesting that you go along with what others are doing?		

Rate your progress: average (A), awesome (AW), or working toward awesome (W).

Chapter 11

Aim High

> If anyone has the courage to take the risks and learn from the failures necessary to discover their passions, talents, values, and sense of destiny—and will then bring their daily activities into alignment with those four internal energy sources—they will have discovered a foundational secret of self-motivation.
>
> —DAVE ARCH, LINCOLN, NE

The ballad "I Believe I Can Fly" is a masterpiece. The song crosses cultural, gender, ethnic, racial, and generational lines. It's a motivational speaker's anthem, lyric after lyric, verse after verse of personal empowerment. The way this world is configured, if you're not making it happen, you're either watching it happen or wondering what happened. To make it happen, you have to believe you can fly!

What prevents people from flapping their wings? Children believe they can fly until they are socialized into a world of self-imposed—and society-imposed—limitations and doubt. Some children wake up in the morning and go to bed at night to wing-clipping choruses of "you can't do this and you can't do that." You cannot consistently perform in a manner that is inconsistent with what you believe.

My mother gave me my wings a long time ago when she said, "Jimmy, you can be whatever it is you want to be as long as you always give your best and never give up." I now believe I can fly because

- I have faith in my God.
- I believe in me.
- I don't believe that we were put on this Earth to fail.
- I'm a true romantic.
- I view life as one continuous journey.
- I know other people believe in me.
- I've cleared a number of life's challenging hurdles.
- I have an incredible support system.
- I know how to bounce back when I fly into negative vectors.
- I've seen what happens when you're disciplined and determined.
- I'm committed to being awesome.

My daughter Daecia is now getting her wings, too; I savor watching her flap and grow into them. She's a sensational student (at Haddonfield Friends School), pianist, ballerina, and soccer player.

When I left my first employer after nine years to work for another prestigious firm, many of my colleagues thought I was insane. I had been promoted into management (the organization's minority management numbers were low at the time), was well thought of by people at all levels, and was a mentor and role model for many people of color. Working in staff training and development had afforded me the opportunity to travel to our offices across the country, so I had been able to establish an extremely

AWESOME
ADVICE

Growing up in West Texas, my dream of seeing the ocean seemed as remote as a college education, a fulfilling career, a nice home, or a happy marriage. I always wondered if the waves really sounded like what you hear when you put a shell to your ear. I wondered if people actually lived the perfect lives that I saw on television. And I longed for a better life, just as I longed to feel the sand between my toes.

Through my dreaming and believing and finally doing, I saw the ocean for the first time when I was 19. I stood on the shore with the sound of the sea echoing in my head and the grit of the beach on my feet. I was overwhelmed, excited, and a little afraid. At that moment, I realized the world was full of endless possibilities if you *believed*. And just as I made my way to the beach, I *have* achieved many of the things I never thought possible. I often visit the beach now for reflection and more dreaming.

—Trina Crockett, Austin

large network. "Jim, you have it made, why would you leave?" they wondered out loud. "I Believe I Can Fly" had not been written at that point, but I believed I could fly on to other challenges. "See, in life," the Reverend Tamieka Moore says, "it's not that we aim high and miss. . . . What happens is that we aim low and hit."

My departure from my next employer was similar. I was working for a revered company performing extremely well in the financial arena. The organization was boiling over with creative, intelligent, dedicated professionals, and there were not many people of color in key leadership positions. I had an outstanding boss, a leadership position, and a solid reputation. Confused and disillusioned, many of my colleagues confronted me with questions and comments: "Why are you going to leave us? Nobody leaves this company. We're a great firm. What about your partnership? Why leave this safe, suburban environment for what you will get in downtown Philadelphia?" Some considered my move to the city to be a significant step *down*, and they weren't shy in expressing that opinion. Nevertheless, I believed I could fly.

When, after 18 months, I left my vice president position in the city to begin a full-time consulting career with a black-owned diversity and management development firm, you guessed it— more of the same. People openly questioned why I would leave a secure job so quickly. I had been there a little less than two years. Why would I walk away from the huge corner office and a leadership position? Why? I had an entrepreneurial spirit and an intense desire to fly.

The company had been acquired, and I had been offered a similar position with the new organization. But I wanted to soar, to flap my wings. My unwavering desire to move closer to running my own consulting and motivational speaking firm moved me to say goodbye to my vice president's title, my vice president's letterhead, my vice president's business cards, and my classy vice president's corner office with the huge windows (ouch!).

Before I totally flew the coop and soared into running my own company, I experienced a series of suburban/city and corporate/ consulting firm workplace differences that served as potholes along my journey to awesome. Nevertheless, I sensed that these speed bumps in the road would later lead to smoother travels.

I had not anticipated the tremendous difference between working in the suburbs, as I did for the first 12 years of my career, and working in the city. The corporate head games were the same, but the people were different. (OK, here come a ton of generalizations.) My city colleagues were more "street-smart," more stern, walked faster, and had a different edge to them. Their energy was different. Their conversations were different. The atmosphere was totally different! In the suburbs, I'd become used to seeing people sitting on benches, jogging, or walking, and I had even observed wildlife during lunch. In the city, I was now up close and personal with street vendors (selling Chinese food, fruit, CDs, pretzels, hotdogs, newspapers, and more), shoppers, politicians, homeless people, police officers, protesters, activists, and news reporters. I was surrounded by department stores and traffic instead of trees and hiking trails. With regard to the employee makeup, my new company had more diversity than my previous one, and their 10 years' worth of diversity initiatives signaled to me that they were more serious about leveraging all their talent. I adjusted to the change, but the differences were startling.

Consider This: "We learn the rope of life by untying the knots." —Author unknown

Initially, I found life to be vastly different working for my first black-owned firm. I certainly was not used to being in the majority. I felt like I could truly and totally be myself and finally take off the tight assimilation suit I'd worn for so long. For once, I actually had something in common with the CEO and managing partner, and it wasn't just gender and a love for sports.

I guess that because I was now in the majority, I felt a new, fresh sense of empowerment and support. I ceased calculating when to raise my hand or my voice during staff meetings. I did not feel as though I was always being judged. I did not feel management cared about the type of car I drove or the neighborhood I lived in. I felt that I could now talk to think, rather than having to always think before I talked. Moreover, I did not have that "walking-on-eggshells-keep-your-guard-up-at-all-times" corporate feeling I had grown accustomed to lugging around every day.

After nearly two years of full-time diversity consulting with this organization, I believed I could fly again—this time, however, on my own. Everything I did for them I believed I could do on my own. I had learned how to sell, how to manage client relationships, and how to run a consulting practice, but I had also learned that I wanted more *diversity* in my assignments. I remember my private conversations with Barry and Peggy (two members of the leadership team) about my desire to be a motivational speaker and author. I told them I wanted to travel around the world speaking and coaching. Shortly after those revealing conversations, I started JIMPACT Enterprises, Inc. They both said that they wanted to see me fly.

The black-owned consulting firm's second guessers weren't as plentiful; the company was made up of a small collection of individual entrepreneurs and former corporate leaders. In addition, the company was considerably smaller than the larger corporations I had worked for previously. But I did believe that some of my former co-workers were waiting to be able to say, "I told you so."

They nearly got their wish. The year 2000, Y2K, was a brutal one for me professionally. I believe that the general economic downturn played a role. The numerous consulting and speaking opportunities I had lined up disappeared faster than the water

AWESOME ADVICE

I have seen the value of developing a willingness to take risks. Having fearful thoughts about doing something that is new or that has some personal risk associated with it is normal. But guess what? We can change our thoughts if we put our mind to work! As Susan Jeffers says in her book *I Feel the Fear and Do It Anyway!*: "What I find more times than not is that the fear was not justified . . . it was just in my mind. The rewards for jumping out of my comfort zone were great!"

—Joe Sparacino, Philadelphia

in a marathoner's bottle after the race. Business and prospecting calls went unreturned. Proposals were declined and ignored, and I have to admit, second thoughts started flashing through my mind.

My wife, Pat, and I were lying in bed watching a movie on some cable channel one night when the screen went blank, except for the message that reminded me that my cable payment was late. How embarrassing, I thought. But part of me got juiced over this bittersweet experience. I couldn't wait to use this anecdote in one of my sessions! I knew that eventually everything would turn around and I would be flying again. How could I pump up and challenge people to live their dreams, in spite of their perceived roadblocks, if I had not experienced any pain and hardships myself? How could I candidly tell people that fire is hot if I had not been burned myself? And that's been my routine. Endure the mishap, move on with even more vigor, then share the story with others to inspire them to get busy!

Occasional subcontracting work with several consulting and training firms were my parachutes until my own business began to pick up. I did not have to play hide-and-go-seek with the creditors anymore. My bank was undoubtedly disappointed because my monthly bounced-check contributions were going to cease. And I was going to be able to keep a filled gas tank. I've always kidded with others that my barometer for being financially awesome is when the yellow/orange gas gauge light in my SUV (indicating that my gas tank was nearly empty) never comes on again. I believed I could fly.

Today JIMPACT Enterprises has taken off. We have our wings, and the winds of commerce are moving in our favor. Speaking and consulting engagements are now a reality and not just wishful thinking. From Atlanta to Amsterdam, Detroit to Dublin, we have done work both domestically and internationally. I believe a large part is due to my belief that I can fly. I believe that whatever happens, as long as I believe in my God and myself, and have the support of my Titans, I will soar!

Previous successes help steady and strengthen our wings, too, as well as the timing of our next flight. Unfortunately, many don't even consider flying to be a possibility. I read a business periodical a couple of years ago that suggested 85 percent of workers are in jobs they don't like. The study went on to say that 80 percent are in jobs where they only utilize 20 percent of their skill sets each day. That's comparable to having a BlackBerry or cellphone and only knowing how to operate the on, off, and send buttons. That's called underemployment.

I believe professionals in the medical industry have determined that more heart attacks occur on Monday than on any other day of the week. Do you suppose that has anything to do with the number of people who dislike their jobs? How quickly do you think their weekends fly by? Can you imagine consistently working five days to live two? These are the folks who greet you on Monday mornings with a barely audible "hello," then follow that up with a vociferous, "I can't wait for the weekend to get here!"

Why do we settle for average? Why don't we believe we can fly? Why don't we believe we can touch the sky? I know we think about it every night and day—to spread our wings and fly away. We have to believe that we can soar to a better tomorrow.

Moving from Average to Awesome

This chapter is not only about taking risks. It's also about how vital it is to teach others the practice of raising their performance bar early and often. This exercise will help you move from an average mindset to a more positive and powerful awesome way of living.

First, consider which statement describes how you think about pursuing your greatness:

- **Average:** You settle for situations, either professional or personal, that you're not happy with. You watch things happen.
- **Awesome:** You read books on empowerment and living one's dreams. You take risks! You believe in yourself! You make things happen! And you surround yourself with other fliers.

Now, take some time and consider the questions below. Respond to the questions and be sure to explain your answers. Finally, rate yourself on your progress. If you are currently average, say so (A). If you feel you deserve an awesome rating, indicate that as well (AW). If you are neither average nor awesome but working toward being awesome, just write W.

Getting to Awesome

Key questions	Your response and explanation	Rating
Do you let fear and/or the "unknown" slow your momentum when it comes to taking risks?		
Are you currently in a job or situation that you don't like? Have you complained nonstop about this dilemma yet not decided on an exit strategy?		
Do you routinely put yourself in situations that will test your abilities and stretch you?		

Rate your progress: average (A), awesome (AW), or working toward awesome (W).

Chapter 12

Don't Expect Everyone to Applaud Your Awesome Efforts

> I don't place too much emphasis on what others think of me; being respectful and kind to others, letting go of the past and the things I cannot change, are far more important.
>
> —TINA M. GREENE, BINGHAMTON, NY

I can easily recall many of the valuable lessons my mother and grandmothers poured into my head over the years. Unfortunately, my brain must have been on vacation when they warned me that not everyone was going to like me—and how their dislike could affect me, if I let it. I completely missed that one.

Like most teens who endured acne, high-water pants, awful plaid-and-stripe combinations, braces, jokes about weird-looking body parts, parent-contrived haircuts, and fashion statements, I, too, dealt with verbal accosting by friends and classmates on a semiregular basis. Call it kids being kids, or kids having bought into the gross societal stereotypes and distortions about their race (that is, internalized racism), or kids with way too much time on their hands. I can remember nonstop moments of "busting" (making fun of each other).

My three main tormentors in seventh and eighth grade were "Jelly Belly" Jesse Johnson, Walter "Let Go of My Eggo" Taylor, and Anthony "The Slope" Carter. They regularly used to call me "Lipton" because they said my bottom lip weighed a ton. And when that phrase about "loose lips sink ships" became popular, the James Smith lips bull's-eye got even wider. According to my friends, my lips could sink everything from the *Titanic* to the entire U.S. Navy. Somewhat frustrated at one point, I even asked my mom if I could get lip reduction surgery.

None of us understood at the time how deeply we had bought into mainstream standards of beauty and how this kind of teasing had a negative impact on our self-esteem.

With regard to courting, relationships, raging hormones, and girls, I survived those too. I somehow managed to make it through my teen years even though I received my share of "No, thank you, I'm not interested" responses. But that was just a part of the growing-up, character-building process. My world then was not colored with poor self-esteem, negativity, or doubt—just dogged determination.

Yet that "doubt" needle did move back and forth a bit in college and then fluctuated (EKG-like) more dramatically when I entered corporate America in 1984. Initially as a marketing copywriter and then as a corporate trainer, I began an indefatigable mission to get my co-workers, colleagues, and management members to like me and to respect me—in that order. Why? I would discover the answer later.

At first I thought I was merely being respectful, just doing the right thing, going out of my way to help people whenever and however I could. That's what I remembered my mother doing. If someone needed me, I would stay late and come in early, even when I didn't want to. Friendly? I gave more compliments than a smitten suitor. My "other-people-stuff to-do" list outnumbered the days Gilligan spent on the island. I did not realize that while I was accumulating a lot of friends, I was losing a lot of personal and professional power.

Consider This: "Great spirits have always violent opposition from mediocre minds."
—Albert Einstein

Then things got even worse!

When I first became a trainer, I would huddle up with the evaluations at the session's conclusion. If one person out of the 20 attendees gave the session a low score, I would be incredibly disappointed. It didn't matter if the other 19 thought that I walked on water. No, this did not have anything to do with me being a perfectionist; I wanted everyone to like me, to think that I was the most accomplished and friendliest corporate trainer on the planet. Moreover, it may have been a carryover from my middle-school and college days, my yearning for acceptance in a world where I was part of the minority.

I'd beat myself up over one disgruntled person. I'd make changes to the content and the facilitator's manual. I'd change my opener or alter my closing. If the one or two people who'd scored the session only a "good" had left contact information on the evaluation form, I'd call them to arrange a meeting to discuss what I could have done differently. It didn't matter that my sessions continued to receive the most positive evaluations and accolades in my department; I was becoming an overreacting people-pleaser.

How did I finally change? Enter Jeanne Bray. Jeanne, my manager at the time, gave me one of those "developmental opportunity" projects. She challenged me to develop a workshop on assertiveness. That six-month journey changed my life forever. I learned a tremendous amount about my inner self and my inner drive. Through this journey, I learned how I was perceived by others; about positive, powerful, influential language; and about how to teach people how to treat me.

I also used this deep research period of my life to get more involved with my organization's Minority Interchange Group (an affinity and leadership group for minority professionals) and to accumulate important information about my group identity and self-esteem in corporate America.

Through my digging, I discovered numerous professional realities and challenges that are germane to everyone (for example, dealing with stress, corporate politics, managing personal and professional responsibilities, managing issues of self-esteem, and goal setting). I also uncovered professional pointers that, while helpful to the majority, could be much more challenging and laborious for African Americans and other people of color in the workplace (for example, pointers on corporate image, thinking style, appearance pitfalls, networking, managing one's personal life, obtaining informal mentors, acquiring information, marketing one's skills, and survival tips).

Before my rebirth, many of my words and actions were noncommittal, or what I thought people wanted to hear.

The keys to my evolution were these lessons in assertiveness:

All changes begin with a change in your self-concept; believe that you can change your outer reality of life by changing your inner beliefs and attitudes:

- People feed off your confidence.
- You become the person you think, dream, and write about.

- Your dominant thoughts will attract into your life the people and circumstances you need, when and in the form you need them.
- Start making affirming statements like, "I think," "I believe," "I will," and "I will not."
- Constantly feed your mind with the images, words, thoughts, information, and aspirations you desire.
- There are distinct differences between assertiveness, aggression, and passivity; part of being assertive is knowing when not to be.

I love collecting motivational quotes, and I recently came across four quotes that, like an Andrea Bocelli aria, were music to my ears:

- All the water in the sea cannot sink a ship unless the ship has a leak in it.
- The true self is always in motion like music, a river of life, changing, moving, failing, suffering, learning, shining.
- Many would rather be ruined by praise than saved by criticism.
- We cannot become what we need to be by remaining what we are.

I was evolving, but that did not mean that I wouldn't be tested again.

During my last corporate job, I had to fire someone. Leigh worked as a training coordinator on my team. She was a warm and affable person, but when it came to consistent workplace performance, let's just say she was closer to average than she was to awesome. After a number of critical mistakes, late arrivals, "dropped balls," extended lunches, and marathon personal telephone calls, I spoke to her at length about what needed to happen for her to keep her job. During that meeting and subsequent one-to-one meetings, she promised me that she would quickly turn things around. Making matters worse for her was the fact that my management peers were forming a "get rid of Leigh" posse. Every time she made a mistake that had an impact on the department, their cries grew louder and louder.

I consulted with human resources. I consulted with some of my Titans. I talked with my boss, who kept saying that I had to consider the negative impact Leigh was having on the entire department. Sometime during all those conversations, I realized why I was finding it so tremendously difficult to let her go: My people-pleasing tendencies were resurfacing; and she was a black single parent raising a little boy on a modest salary. Some of the thoughts running through my mind included

- We were in the holiday season. Could I hold off the firing squad until the new year?
- My mother had successfully handled a number of single-parent challenges as she raised my brother and me. Could Leigh step up to this one?
- Why had no one addressed this situation before? Leigh joined the department before I did. Why was this situation left for the new guy, me, to handle? Could Leigh's race have played a factor? Or did people think she would say that her race was the reason people consistently questioned her performance?

After some deep thinking and another very serious one-to-one meeting, I gave Leigh one more chance. I emphatically explained to her how close she was to losing her job, that I had done all that I could conceivably do or would do. Two days later, she took three hours for lunch to get her hair done. The next day, December 15, I fired her. I thought about her little boy. I thought about her bills. I thought about the upcoming holidays. I thought about her future. But I also knew that I had to hold her accountable. Nevertheless, this entire episode still bothers me.

Occasionally, since then, I've had to manage other gut-checking moments during my journey. And although I have plenty of training and education under my belt, I have not yet graduated from life. As Ralph Waldo Emerson wrote, "The hero is the person who is immovably centered." That immovable center allows everything around it to move freely but provides an anchor.

My anchor is put to the test during many of the diversity sessions I lead. After one challenging diversity workshop that targeted race, I wrote an article titled "Malcolm, Martin, and Tom: The Three Faces of a Black Male Diversity Consultant," which was published in the *Next Step* diversity magazine. What made the session so exasperating was that, after spending eight hours trying to support and protect the only white participants (three white females) in the room (there were six black participants), I was crushed when I read their session evaluations. To paraphrase their comments, they said I was confrontational, out of touch, and there to start trouble.

The premise of my *Next Step* article was that it didn't make a difference what I said, what I wore, how much I smiled; certain people were going to view me as either Malcolm X, Dr. Martin Luther King Jr., or Uncle Tom. Here is a sample of what I wrote:

> Over the years, I've had countless rewarding sessions with white audiences. We've laughed, cried and brainstormed many ways to leverage diversity in their organizations and in their personal lives. We've even, to an extent, explored race. The gold bracelet I wear on my left wrist during diversity sessions is a thank-you gift from a white male participant—his way of showing appreciation for my opening his eyes to aspects of diversity he had never considered before. But it's the painful, afflictive sessions that I unfortunately lose sleep over.

AWESOME ADVICE

As a human resources manager who is consistently dealing with disgruntled employees who just don't believe they should have to work to receive a salary, I'm always dealing with drama. At times, I'm viewed as the bad cop. That's why I really put a lot of emphasis on those who truly appreciate their jobs. I have taken to writing thank-you notes to those associates just to remind them that they are doing a great job and to keep up the awesome work. The notes make a huge difference to the associates, and their energy helps make it possible for me to deal positively with the employees who don't think I'm so awesome.

—Adrianne Winter, San Ramon, CA

Evaluations from those episodes cause me to wonder if I ever will be totally judged by the content of my character and my ability and not by the color of my skin. Some of my positive evaluations have drippings of stereotyping too. They say, "He was great and non-threatening." Who said I was going to be threatening? These are subliminal stereotypes trick-or-treating as positive evaluative remarks. If my agenda were to grind a race ax, then I would probably understand the emotional, pointed feedback better. Besides, confrontational, minority diversity consultants are as welcome as line dancing at a chess tournament.

Some blacks have viewed me as a sell-out because they associate my words of optimism and encouragement with words of compromise and assimilation. They expect me to repetitiously validate the contention that they've been dogged by "the white man," and to publicly blame the institutional systems, structures, and cultures they stomach everyday. When I don't present the facts as strongly as they'd like, I sense that they believe I'm all fluff and no stuff. If they feel I'm not pushing hard enough, they will take it upon themselves to turn up the volume. That's when I find myself playing lifeguard, monitoring the amount of time everyone (that is, blacks, whites, Latinos, Asians, Hispanics, Native Americans) spends in the "race pool" conversation.

. . . I find this journey to be incredibly challenging, exhausting, moving, yet rewarding. I wonder if I ever will be seen as someone other than Malcolm, Martin or Tom?

Despite these challenges, I still have a job to do: to help *all* people move from average to awesome. I now travel nationally and internationally, meeting thousands of people, facilitating hundreds of workshops and doing motivational speaking. I'm in the zone. I'm the artist. Through my work, I passionately paint the picture and then stand back. Many people gasp with appreciation while others move on to the next painting (going back to their previous stressful life routines). Nevertheless, as long as I remain positive, centered, and assertive, and believe I've done my best, I always win. I cannot be awesome if I'm always worrying about what other people think. Besides, some people are just not going to clap anyway. And that's OK.

Moving from Average to Awesome

This chapter is not only about avoiding becoming a people pleaser. It's also about how you have to develop a solid interior—one that doesn't succumb to criticism, constructive feedback, or dislike. This exercise will help you move from an average mindset to a more positive and powerful awesome way of living.

First, consider which statement describes how you think about others' opinions of you:

- **Average:** You are overly concerned with what people think of you and your ability. You overreact when someone doesn't like you or like what you've done.
- **Awesome:** You're developing an extremely strong, positive self-concept and affirming group identity. You're staying centered and remembering that your beliefs become your reality. You know what your special sensitivities are and are working hard to not let anyone get to you.

Second, take some time and consider the questions below. Respond to the questions and be sure to explain your answers. Finally, rate yourself on your progress. If you are currently average, say so (A). If you feel you deserve an awesome rating, indicate that as well (AW). If you are neither average nor awesome but working toward being awesome, just write W.

Getting to Awesome

Key questions	Your response and explanation	Rating
Do you avoid putting yourself in uncomfortable or unfamiliar situations and then make excuses for why you did?		
Do you routinely make disparaging or "put-down" comments about yourself?		
Do you spend unnecessary time worrying about how others think about you?		

Rate your progress: average (A), awesome (AW), or working toward awesome (W).

Chapter 13

Be Yourself—Everyone Else Is Taken

> Be true to yourself, your values, and your ideas. Strive to make a difference no matter how small. Always be someone who adds value to a situation or relationship—not someone who detracts from it. Always, always maintain your integrity and dignity.
>
> —SHERRY NOTTINGHAM, PHILADELPHIA

I once asked my ex-wife to give me an example of when she felt as though she wasn't being true to herself. Without hesitation, she said when she felt pressure to be somebody she wasn't, just to make someone else happy. I continued my inquiry. "How did that make you feel?" "I didn't like it. . . . I felt phony and, depending how phony I was being, I felt pretentious, . . . just not good about myself," she said.

Over the years, I've met quite a few impostors, pretenders, and quick-change artists—people who are seldom themselves. Clearly there are times when we all feel pressured to pretend to be someone we're not. For whatever reason (fame, fear, survival, greed, love, low self-esteem, collusion, corporate pressures), we can lose sight of the "To thine own self be true" mantra. Here are some of the folks I've met professionally and personally who subscribe to an "updated" version of this mantra—"To thine own self be you." Have you met any of them?

Em U. Late: These people want to be like Mike, striving to mirror the efforts, style, and/or mannerisms of their hero or heroine. They dress, walk, talk, dance, and yearn to perform and behave similarly. Being in the "say for pay" profession myself, I have a keen eye for speakers who shamelessly copy the routines, quips, quotes, gestures, delivery, and movements of other speakers. And if they're not already thinking about cloning their idol, others push their "copy cat" snowball down the hill: "He's going to be the next [Letterman, Ali, Poitier]" or "She's going to be the next [Nadia, Tyra, Aretha]," they offer. Several years ago, Nike even got the "I'm Tiger Woods" bandwagon rolling for a group of young impressionables.

Wyle Atwork: Many admit they act differently while at work than they do at home. Over the years, Wyle has come to realize that what gets rewarded gets repeated—and then gets rewarded again. Wyle is a quick study, assessing and then performing similarly to those in his or her corporation. Because many of today's organizations are conservative, bottom-line, and results oriented, Wyles usually work in corporate environments where these four factors tend to be at play:

- Work is primarily a goal-oriented activity.
- Power involves positions of authority and control of financial resources.
- Problem solving tends to focus on tasks and quick results, not necessarily on processes and people.

- Elitism, status, and titles are used as measures to value others.

Pretty soon, Wyles' walk, talk, dress, work style, companions, and interests change. The frustrated Wyles that I've met continually work to survive, evolve, and fit in. This has a higher price when one's personal or cultural style is further from the corporate standard. Nearly every part of his or her day is spent trying to perfect this corporate identity and shuffle. Wyles, over time, usually move from one organization to the next, until they soar, settle, or start their own businesses. As a recovering Wyle, I learned that you can only pretend for so long. The costume eventually has to come off.

Pierre Pressure: These people just want to fit in with their peer group and do whatever they must to fit in. They want to do "it" because that's what everyone else is doing. Changing their looks, their diet, their field of study, their exercise routine, their socializing habits, and their interests are at the top of their lists. To fit in, they are prone to falsehoods and exaggeration. Eventually they grow tired of running on this uphill treadmill. They become remorseful, unfulfilled, and depressed.

B. A. Jones: This person lives to keep up with the other Joneses. It's mostly a materialistic mission. From automobiles to SUVs, from houses to decks, from desktop computers to laptop computers, from Palm Pilots to pagers, from VCRs to DVDs, from coats to clothes, from season tickets to timeshares, B. A. labors to duplicate and will go to ridiculous lengths to keep pace.

You'd better buy a security system for your accomplishments, as they are also fair game. B. A. Jones will attend the same schools, major in the same subjects, join the same organizations and associations, take up the same hobbies, and even work out at the same sports clubs.

Hal Others-Seemee: Hal, bless his heart, merely wants to put a smile on your face. Hal spends his life striving to live up to your expectations of him. Denying the interests, activities, and pursuits that bring him joy, Hal will jump through fiery hoops to please you. On numerous occasions, I've heard a Hal say he did something because someone else wanted him to. Somewhere along his journey, Hal forgot who he was. Hals change majors, change occupations, change partners, and change their minds because you want them to. If you know a Hal, please share these two thoughts with him: "You were born an original; don't be a copy" (Rich Meiss) and "When we are unable to find tranquillity within ourselves, it is useless to seek it elsewhere" (La Rochefoucauld).

Consider This: "Change is a door that can only be opened from the inside."
—Terry Neil

Sherry Nottingham and I worked together at my last full-time job. My office was at one end of the floor and hers at the other end, but our outlook on life, passions, and interests created a space for us to develop a beautiful friendship. We often talked about diversity (Sherry is Japanese American), work-family balance, and what it takes to be truly happy and fulfilled. During a recent conversation, Sherry (now a mother of three who left the corporate chaos to begin a family) said that being self-motivated drives her to be the person she is: "I have an inner drive; much of my motivation comes from within, so my competition is within myself to be the best that I possibly can be at all times and with all people with whom I come in contact.

"Having said that, I do my best to be true to myself, my values, and my ideals. I live by the rule that we model the behavior that we would like to see others share in our presence (trust,

AWESOME
ADVICE

While I am truly content with being me, I am even more a willful visionary. So to accept that who and where I am in life is all that was meant to be would be to deny my vision, which is something greater than the whole of me, and would only serve to keep me comfortably stuck. As I grow, I find it important to be gentle with myself and to appreciate where I began this lifelong journey on the road to awesome.

One of the greatest motivators in reaching new heights is the intrinsic belief that I am worth it. The idea that I am a valuable, capable, and lovable human being was personally a hard sell for many years, but by surrounding myself with people who were able to see and validate the beauty I possess, I eventually gained total buy-in, and was then able to radiate it beyond myself to benefit others.

Ultimately, what makes it all good and keeps me positive is all about perspective. I have the power to redefine any barrier or situation based on how I choose to perceive it and receive it.

—Kimberly Cortijo, Davis, CA

honesty, integrity, and so on) as opposed to simply lecturing about the merits of such behavior. I strive for inner peace and nurture my spirit in part by knowing that every day when I look at myself in the mirror and when I go to sleep at night I can live with myself. Life presents many challenges with no right or wrong answers, . . . where the lines are not clear and often are fuzzy and gray. Knowing, however, in my gut that I did the right thing as opposed to the popular thing is so much easier than struggling with the conflict of going against my heart and my gut."

You will not move from average to awesome if your life's quest is to pretend to be a person you're not. Love yourself. Take care of yourself. Be yourself, because everyone else is taken!

Moving from Average to Awesome

This chapter is not only about developing your own identity. It's also about how easy it is to lose sight of who you are and fall prey to social, organizational, affinity group, political, individual, cultural, and other influences. This exercise will help you move from an average mindset to a more positive and powerful awesome way of living.

First, consider which statement describes how you think about your level of self-understanding and self-actualization:

- **Average:** You're living a life using other people's thoughts, perceptions, and beliefs as your measuring stick.
- **Awesome:** You're developing your own identity and becoming the best possible YOU you can be. You've bought a mirror and hung it somewhere near the front door—and you're now looking in the mirror every day before you head out into the world, to remind yourself that you're awesome and that you're going to be true to yourself.

Second, take some time and consider the questions below. Respond to the questions and be sure to explain your answers. Finally, rate yourself on your progress. If you are currently average, say so (A). If you feel you deserve an awesome rating, indicate that as well (AW). If you are neither average nor awesome but working toward being awesome, just write W.

Getting to Awesome

Key questions	Your response and explanation	Rating
Do you make personal changes without checking multiple sources?		
Who do you wish you were more like? Why?		
What has driven the personal changes you've recently made?		

Rate your progress: average (A), awesome (AW), or working toward awesome (W).

Chapter 14

Play the Hand You're Dealt

> You can have horrible things happen to you, and I have. But I have never let my past keep me down. I deal with it and I'm completely resilient. I always hold my head up and move forward faster and stronger.
>
> —NANCY REBECCA, CHICAGO

Raise your right hand, right at this moment, if you've ever worked for a miserable manager. Stand up, right now, if you've ever worked in a lousy company. If you've ever felt that life was not fair, say to yourself, "Been there, done that; I've got the T-shirt and the hat."

Obviously, we're not always dealt the best hand or provided the best possible circumstances. What's significant—and I'm sure this will not be the first time you've heard this—is it's how you play your hand that counts.

Former Philadelphia high school coach and physical education teacher Steve Kane's playing cards were "The Bottom." That's what we called the West Philadelphia neighborhood where my high school, University City, was located. The students who attended the school were a combination of the gifted and the gritty. We had bookworms and bookies, scholars and schemers, the tough and the talented.

Steve coached the boys' tennis and girls' volleyball teams. For 27 years, he was also the boys' basketball coach. This father of three and grandfather of five also became the adopted white father of nearly every black ballplayer who ever donned the Jaguars black and gold basketball uniform. During his years with the school, Steve's reality was the kind of black, urban drama captured in Spike Lee and John Singleton movies. Every year Steve tangled with gang violence, single-parent families, drugs, poverty, robberies, homelessness, and low SAT scores.

Along with the obligatory college recruiting visits, the on- and off-court coaching, mentoring, and tutoring, Coach Steve's unofficial job description included delivering eulogies, providing bail money and rides home, buying clothes for his players, visiting wounded players' bedsides, interrupting drug deals, and providing meals. His responsibilities extended beyond high school as he mentored many of his players while they pursued college degrees. He was in the stands at many of my college football games, coached me through the rigors of attending a predominantly white university, and convinced me to buy my first pair of Docksiders. He also found time to win 347 games, coach numerous playoff teams, and win the high school Public League Basketball Championship in 1995.

Upon joining the University City faculty in 1972, Steve found a predominantly black, inner-city school with lower- to lower-middle-class students, a lack of facilities and school tradition, and recurring gang violence. Considering the situation, he could have lobbied for an assignment in a more white, affluent, suburban environment. Time after time when his players' predicaments took precedence over his own personal life challenges, he could have packed his gym bag, put on his coat and hat, and left. No one would have blamed him if he had transferred to a more prominent school, one that at least had its own football field. I remember those days where all of us—the varsity and junior varsity football teams, girls' field hockey teams, and boys' soccer teams—practiced simultaneously on the same 50-yard-long dirt hill called a field. However, until he retired in 1999, Steve played the hand he was dealt. And he played it extremely well. My teammates and other alumni loved him for it. He was even adopted by the residents of the "The Bottom" as their coach.

My brother once had a peculiar hand to play, too. He had graduated from the University of Pittsburgh in 1987 with a degree in psychology and sought to obtain an MBA with a focus on international business. There were five immediate concerns, however. One, money. Two, money. Three and four, money. Five, there weren't many schools that offered the special, accelerated curriculum Rodney desired. He handled the fifth concern by choosing the University of Hartford.

Next, he had to wrestle, flip, take down, and pin the other four concerns. Oh, I left out one additional factor. Hartford informed him that part of his MBA coursework would involve completing the first year's curriculum in Paris. I remember my mother looking at my brother's playing cards and cringing because of what she saw.

This was his hand: (1) To pay for the year in France, he had to send his student loan money overseas and have it exchanged for French currency; (2) until that money arrived, he would only have enough money to fly to Paris and live for a couple of days; (3) even with the student loan, he would not have enough money to return home; (4) the only French he knew was "Voulez-vous coucher avec moi ce soir?" (thanks, Patti LaBelle); (5) he hadn't secured a place to stay, and without the money from the loan, he couldn't afford to pay rent; and (6) he was the only African American in his international business class of 50.

My mother, who is as cautious and risk-averse as they come, did not appreciate my cheering, "Go, Rod, Go! Go, Rod, Go!" from the sidelines.

Rodney looked at his hand one more time, then started playing it. As soon as he arrived in France, he met an American who had an apartment for rent. The guy, coincidentally, was from the same Philadelphia neighborhood where we had moved when we left my Dad. Hearing the financial dilemma Rodney was in, the man let him live rent-free for awhile. The "while" turned into "some time."

This was fantastic, but then Rodney's cards got worse.

After two months of nonpayment, the school informed Rodney that if he were to continue in the program they would have to receive his tuition soon. That "soon" became two weeks. In the midst of this, however, his cards finally began to improve. His survival instincts and amiable personality enabled him to connect and build relationships with his classmates. Those relationships grew to the point where he was never in a situation where he had to worry about a meal, a study partner, or a glass of wine. He also learned enough French to get by.

Rodney's student loan money arrived at last. The school got its tuition. The supportive landlord got his rent. And in 18 months, my brother got his MBA in international business from the University of Hartford. Yes, he played his cards just right—but it wasn't easy.

"Major frustration," Rodney said, as he recounted the entire experience to me. "I wish that a non-sports-related analogy came to mind but it doesn't, so here it is. There were a number of obstacles, but to put it simply, I was a road team playing without its best players. The road was Paris, I was the team and my best players were my resources, my family, my friends, my language, my familiar housing and living conditions. And in the beginning I thought that I was going to win by attending Drexel University [in Philadelphia]. Everything would have been familiar to me. Shortly after I began the Hartford MBA Program (because of the international experience and the accelerated degree program), I began to view the France experience much differently. I played to survive. I felt that if I had my resources, I would have been able to perform much, much better. I wasn't used to playing to keep the score close. I wasn't used to not going for the A. I found myself going for not failing, taking the sure shots. I decided to keep the score close until we played the second half on my home court in the States. I kept telling myself to hold on. I couldn't get knocked out. I had to hang on for six to nine months until I got home and got my best players back."

Consider This: "It is my belief that talent is plentiful, and that what is lacking is staying power." —Doris Lessing

---

The Russell H. Conwell Middle Magnet (my junior high school) Crew met again during the Christmas holidays a couple of years ago. Every year this group of 1970s Survivors (usually somewhere between eight and ten of us attend) meet for dinner on the last Saturday of the year to check in, catch up, and reminisce. I don't attend the event every year, but when I do, it doesn't take too many minutes before I'm all caught up with everything about everybody.

Our "playing cards" at Conwell had included being a handful of black students attending a predominantly white middle school from 1973 to 1975. The hand appeared sensational on the out-side (that is, attending one of the academically best-rated middle schools in the city), but that's why playing cards have numbers on one side and generic colors on the back. The school was also located in one of the most racially divided, blue-collar areas of Philadelphia. My classmates were my first true affinity group. We protected, coached, tutored, and loved one another—and we survived.

As I sat at the Warmdaddy's restaurant dinner table, I became mesmerized in the moment. The place was packed, the jazz was kicking, and the energy was electric. I looked around the table at Larry Horne and at Jessica Battle, at Tony Spann and at Charles Carr, at Deidre (Graham) Childs and at Vanessa Faire, at Harry Kirby and at David Thomas. Recalling the stories about how we survived the neighborhood thugs, I moved from boisterous laughter to quiet tears.

Life wasn't hilarious or amusing back then. Nearly every day or every other day, we (like many of the Conwell students of color) were assaulted, roughed up, or just barely escaped a severe beating from the white neighborhood toughs. They were the Fight Club, and we were their fodder.

Most of us commuted to school on public transportation. Groups of grade-schoolers (girls and boys, mostly black but also Latino and Asian) walked slowly with schoolbooks in hand through the blue-collar white neighborhood, heading to the train, anticipating at any moment having to run or fight to get to safety. The 10-minute walk from the train to the school seemed like hours.

There was one additional depressing element to this ritual. Whenever the neighborhood white guys beat us up, several of the tough guys in our crew beat up the white neighborhood Catholic school students who were still on the train when we boarded. Those students, their faces signaling trepidation and panic when we boarded the train frustrated and beaten, had to endure five long, drawn-out minutes of accosting and revenge before they reached their stop.

Conwell's annex (used for graphic arts, shop, and home economics) was located two and a half blocks from the main building. Walking back and forth between buildings was our version of Russian roulette. When we traveled in a group alongside our white classmates, the neighborhood bullies and dropouts settled for staring at us and mouthing obscenities. When we traveled alone, we were moving targets. If we were running late for class, let's just say we missed class that day. It was safer that way. Talk about having an awful playing hand. We were 12-year-old, 13-year-old, and 14-year-old students. They were 17-year-old, 18-year-old, 19-year-old, and 20-year-old thugs.

My ex-wife, who had joined us for dinner, asked why we didn't just transfer to another school. As Larry explained, we all listened, nodding in agreement. "Pat, we formed a collective bond, a tight group," he said. "We were getting a great education and we *were* going to make it together."

I sat there, counting my blessings. I've never undervalued the significance of my mentally and physically escaping that racial war zone called a neighborhood. Nevertheless, I had heard these stories before. I had been on the receiving end of a lot of the many punches, kicks, rocks, snowballs, baseball bats, brass knuckles, taunts, and threats. But because I was in the midst of writing this book, I was more reflective, sentimental, and moved. I was proud of my classmates. We all graduated. We all survived. We all played the hand that was in front of us.

When I attended Widener University, I had to play another complicated hand. My cards included a predominantly white university, faculty, and students. Regardless of how many friendships I developed, there were still many times when I felt lonely, with few people to talk to and few people who would understand or want to understand what it felt like to consistently be in the minority. I have many memories from those four years. My highlights: graduating on time with a degree in English; meeting a phenomenal

English professor and mentor, Larry Kelly, who took over where Mrs. Brodie left off; winning a Division III National Championship in football and developing several incredible friendships. My lowlights were many of my card-playing experiences. I recall the time I was returning to my campus apartment after an evening of backgammon with some friends. There was a party going on next door. The door was open and the music was blasting. I took a quick peak inside and made eye contact with one of the gregarious party guests. He invited me up by saying, "Come on in man. We don't smoke ci-gars—we smoke ni-gars."

Part of playing the hand you're dealt is picking up the cards. Working in corporate America for 14 years, I saw and experienced enough inequities to last several lifetimes. My colleagues and I would routinely discuss how unfair corporate life was. Broken promises regarding promotions, jobs given to people without going through the appropriate posting procedures, and tons of natural informal mentoring relationships among white co-workers were the norm. For the most part early on, though, we did more talking about our issues than doing something about them. We stared at our cards rather than playing them.

As a diversity consultant, I travel to companies facilitating one-day to one-week diversity workshops aimed at helping participants excel in this ever-changing workforce. I also provide direction in how to play the corporate hands they've been dealt. During the sessions we discuss and participate in activities and exercises centered on the workforce's changing demographics; equal employment opportunity and affirmative action goals, laws, and regulations; the impact that stereotypes, perceptions, values, beliefs, and collusion have on workplace interactions, synergy, and opportunities; the business reasons for managing diversity; and the significance of self-empowerment.

The self-empowerment discussion is invaluable because sometimes things happen to you that make your head spin more than

AWESOME
ADVICE

I'll never forget the day my dad walked my older brother and me out to the barn. It was the first time I'd ever seen my dad cry. Immediately, I knew something was wrong. David, my younger brother, was very sick. It was cancer. In his small, not-fully-developed five-year-old brain, a tumor the size of a grapefruit was growing.

Over the next three and a half years, David had two brain surgeries, plus radiation and chemotherapy treatments, before finally succumbing to the cancer at the tender age of eight and a half. Never once in that time did I hear him ask, "Why me? Why not some other kid?" Not once did my parents ask, "Why did this happen to our child?"

My family's strength during that time was amazing. My parents tried to make life as normal as possible for us. We did not have health insurance and we had little money. My Mom had taken a leave of absence from work to care for David, and my Dad was away from home a lot.

I did not recognize the significance of what transpired over those three and a half years until much later in life. For many years, we didn't talk about David. As we got older, talking about him became easier; we did it more frequently. As I have matured and have reflected on that period in my life, I have realized that every time I come across a challenging situation, or every time I need a bit of additional strength, I think about David, and I think about my family. They are what get me through. I get strength from them. Knowing what we went through—realizing that my parents watched one of their children die, unable to do much about it—makes one of life's curve balls seem like child's play.

—Kim Schreck, Sacramento

Linda Blair's in *The Exorcist*. Just as Monopoly, The Game of Life, Scrabble, Twister, and Trouble have survived over time, participants adamantly insist that corporate games are still around. And like those board games, the corporate games have also been updated.

Initially, there's often more angry conversation about the cards that have been dealt than the actual playing of the cards. To help them play their hands and clear some of their corporate hurdles, I encourage session attendees to use these Jim's Gems:

- Gem 1: Secure mentors and coaches (of all races, ages, ethnicities, and backgrounds).
- Gem 2: Become outstanding, invaluable, and a specialist in your area by getting additional licenses, experiences, certifications, and coursework.
- Gem 3: Build relationships and align yourself with the appropriate reference groups.
- Gem 4: Work collectively with others to defeat unfair practices both in and outside the workplace.
- Gem 5: Take risks.
- Gem 6: Stop providing the ammunition (that is, the "stuff" that sinks your corporate ship: inappropriate dress, poor punctuality and work habits, improper grammar, weak technology skills, subpar presentation skills).
- Gem 7: Learn and understand your organization's corporate culture.
- Gem 8: Gain exposure throughout the organization through projects, volunteerism, and assignments.
- Gem 9: Be open to feedback, but know your limitations.
- Gem 10: Look for ways to reinvent yourself, and be very slow to play your age, gender, sexual orientation, race, class, or disability card if things are not going your way.

Playing the hand you're dealt builds character and fulfills dreams. It also creates opportunities to acquire wisdom and experience so that you can mentor and coach others. Today, I live to help people create new and improved hands for themselves. The first instructions I give them are to pick up their cards, look at them, and then start playing; that's when the cards begin to change. I remind them that in this card game called life, we can't throw in our cards and hope we're dealt better ones next hand. There is no next hand.

Moving from Average to Awesome

This chapter is not only about adapting and overcoming. It's also about sustainability, courage, and willpower. This exercise will help you move from an average mindset to a more positive and powerful awesome way of living.

First, consider which statement describes how you think about dealing with drama and trials:

- **Average:** You complain about the hand you're dealt. You only do something about your situation when things are rock-bottom low.
- **Awesome:** You're proactive and resilient, earnestly and consistently playing the hand you're dealt. You're incorporating Jim's Gems into your routine.

Second, take some time and consider the questions below. Respond to the questions and be sure to explain your answers. Finally, rate yourself on your progress. If you are currently average, say so (A). If you feel you deserve an awesome rating, indicate that as well (AW). If you are neither average nor awesome but working toward being awesome, just write W.

Getting to Awesome

Key questions	Your response and explanation	Rating
Do you spend more time complaining about your dire situation or doing something about your situation?		
What lessons have you learned from those situations?		
What tension-filled situations do you find yourself in again and again? Does the outcome ever change? Why? How?		

Rate your progress: average (A), awesome (AW), or working toward awesome (W).

Chapter 15

Live with a Forgiving Spirit

I look for the goodness in others. I'm genuinely interested in others, and it's amazing how much I learn and
grow just listening to and engaging with people.

—DELORIS DAVIS, PHILADELPHIA

I was helping my uncle carry a chair down the stairs and out
the front door. We—my mother, brother, and I—were moving. We were leaving my father.

My Dad had a couple of personalities. One was spectacular. He
was the life of every party: witty, charismatic, charming, sensitive,
and poetic. I enjoyed sitting on the living room couch watching
him and my mom jitterbug and bop during one of our family "get
down" nights. Plus he could *sing*! I loved when he sang, "It's a
beautiful morning, I think I'll go outside for awhile. . . ." or "God
didn't make little green apples, and it don't rain in Indianapolis
in the summertime. . ." or "Fly me to the moon and let me play

among the stars. . . ." He taught me how to listen to a baseball game on the radio and keep the scorebook at the same time. My love of sports—that was my Dad's doing also. We used to race (I never did win), play half-ball, and fly kites. That Dad, unfortunately, didn't show up enough.

His other personality would rear its ugly head after he spent time with his after-work buddies. Guzzling adult beverages was their pastime. After making his post-work pit stops, Dad would take the train home. Upon getting off the train, usually appearing very disheveled, he would stagger down the street heading to our home on Sansom Street. The five-minute walk would take him what seemed like hours. From the living room window, I would dejectedly and somberly watch him stagger home. My friends, outside playing, would watch too. They would later do their "Jim's Dad drunk-walking down the street" impersonations when we played.

The times he couldn't get his key in the door, he'd ring our doorbell—until it stopped working. Then he'd just bang on the door with his fist. When he did manage to get his key in the door, he sometimes would come in and sit on the first step; we lived on the second floor of the apartment building. He would take a nap that lasted until the next morning, when it was time for him to go to work again. Other times, he would come upstairs, go straight to the bathroom, and spend the night sleeping on the toilet. Those times when he successfully scaled the 14 steps that led to the hallway, he would, without fail, head to the living room looking behind the sofa, chair, and television set for the bottles of beer, vodka, and/or whiskey that he had hidden. Mom had usually found them first and had flushed them down the toilet. As regular as clockwork, that generally led to an extremely loud argument that at times turned physical.

As I was carrying the chair, I thought about when Mom first told us we were moving. She called my brother and me into the dining room and said, "I have $2,100. We can use this money to buy a house that I've found or we can buy a new car." I asked my Mom if we bought the new house was Dad going to go with us? She said no. My brother Rodney and I hesitated for a moment and then said, "Let's buy the house." The plan began.

We decided to move while my Dad was still at work. Because missing a full day of school wasn't an option, Rodney and I would get an early dismissal. My Mom would take the day off from work to pack, and we'd be gone before my Dad got home from work. I replayed all this in my head as my uncle and I carried the chair down the steps.

When we reached the bottom step to head out the front door to the moving van, my Dad met us. When I looked up, he was directly in front of me. I was as motionless as a mannequin. Angrily, he asked, "Where's your mother?" I looked down. "Where's your mother, Jimmy, what's going on? What are you doing?" Staring at the ground, I mumbled, "We're moving, Daddy, and Mom is upstairs in the kitchen." This was a rare day when Dad had not stopped off on the way home to hang out with his friends. Actually, he had left work early, hoping to spend some happy quality time with his family. There was no sign of alcohol, just the handsome, concerned husband and father of two, James Alvin Smith Sr.

He looked around for a quick second, assessing everything that was going on in front of him, and immediately turned around. He walked down the front steps, around the corner, and out of my life. In the next 25 years, I saw my dad only a handful of times.

I carried a grudge every day for nearly a quarter century.

I played Little League sports. I played sports in high school. I played sports in college. I had several professional football tryouts. No Dad to cheer me on. No Dad to say, "That's my son!" No Dad to break me down, then build me up. No Dad to walk the sidelines, giving the coach "You better put my son in the game" looks.

No Dad to teach me the tricks of the athletic trade. No Dad to talk to about relationships, the birds and the bees, and love. No Dad to teach me how to drive. No Dad to go fishing with. No Dad at my high school graduation. No Dad at my college graduation. No Dad when I received my master's degree. No Dad at my wedding. No Dad at my daughter's birth. My mother wore both hats, and I love her for that. I guess that's why I have a soft spot for single parents.

I did visit my Dad once shortly after we moved. I went to the house after school to check in on him. It was a brief visit, because he said he was heading out; my intuition told me that he wasn't ready to talk about things just yet. I still remember seeing his milk carton, water bottle, and other groceries sitting on the windowsill between the screen and storm windows. Because we had taken the refrigerator, this was his makeshift method for keeping his food fresh. Mom gave him our new address, and he actually stopped by a couple of times with toys, apologetic conversation, and a plea to us to get Mom to take him back. The last time I saw him after that was when he stood on the sidelines, for the first and only time, during one of my Little League football games. What threw me was his traveling companion—a baby boy who I would later find out was my stepbrother Mark. As the game wound down, I looked to the sidelines for my Dad. I had hoped to receive some postgame fatherly feedback. We'd gotten crushed, but I had returned a kick-off for a touchdown. Besides, it was the first time he'd seen me play organized football—uniforms, referees, the whole bit. But he had gone.

During the next 20-plus years, I thought about trying to find my Dad to clear the air, to let bygones be bygones. I discovered that he had remarried and that along with Mark I had a stepsister named Stacy, who was his wife's daughter. I also learned that my Dad still lived in Philadelphia, financially just making it from one day to the next, paycheck to paycheck.

We did walk into the same house a couple of times during family gatherings. We would stare at each other from a distance, looking more for the effects of time and age, never sharing more than a sentence or two. I had become resentful. Our communication consisted of a phone conversation every four or five years. He needed a SWAT team to get into my heart. When he had a mild heart attack, then later a stroke, I, along with Mom and Rodney, went to see him in the hospital. Once we saw that he was going to be fine, we hugged, shook hands, and I departed.

I saw him two other times. Once, I traveled to his West Philadelphia home to introduce him to my first wife on our way to an event in the same neighborhood. That awkward visit lasted about 30 minutes as I facilitated the meeting so that he conversed more with her than with me.

Five years later, when my daughter Daecia was born, I took my little angel and Pat to see him for the first time. Daecia was his first grandchild, and he was thrilled to see her. I gave him her photo, and he promised to stay in touch. But the next time we talked, nearly three years later, he was calling to borrow $100. I mailed him the money, he returned it as promised, and months elapsed before we talked again. After several more calls over a period of months, we agreed to meet for dinner to have a long-anticipated heart-to-heart discussion about our past and our future. Like many of our planned get-togethers, the meeting never took place.

On the morning of our scheduled dinner meeting, my father had a heart attack at work and died. At age 59, James A. Smith Sr. became a more painful memory for me than he ever had been before.

Dad's boss had driven him to work that morning, arriving around 6:00 a.m. Dad was the custodian for a hair salon. When he realized he had forgotten his lunch, his boss volunteered to drive back home to pick it up. When the boss returned, about three hours later, he found my father slumped on the floor. My brother, who was contacted first, called me with the news. I was paralyzed, humbled, and ached all over. I cried. I was really fatherless now.

Those many years of resentment and anger seemed so frivolous. Why hadn't I patched things up? Why hadn't I let go of my bitterness? Why hadn't I just been able to move on? Why couldn't I just have appreciated the fact that I did have a father and worked to develop some semblance of a relationship? Why hadn't I cultivated a forgiving spirit? When I sat inches away from his open coffin during the funeral and then again when I closed the furnace door during his cremation, I was totally distraught, blaming myself for this somber reconciliation. Yes, many people told me that he could have tried to find me, too. But I own a significant piece of that father–son relationship pie, and it still doesn't taste good.

After my father died, I decided that I wanted to do something noteworthy to honor his memory. Both through his charm and personality and through his battle with alcohol, nicotine, and anger, he taught me how to be a man, how to be responsible, and how to be a father—yes, *how* to be a father.

My father's death smacked me with the reality that you should live each day to the fullest because tomorrow is not promised.

I decided to start using "Jr." after my name. For the first 38 years of my life, I was called James Smith, Jimmy Smith, or Jim Smith, but never Jim Smith Jr. So after May 9, 1999, I began taking my father, through the use of "Jr.," everywhere I went. It was a very small gesture that turned into a wonderful tribute to the man I now think about every day. As a speaker, I'm introduced or I have the opportunity to introduce myself quite often. Now, in front of audiences of all sizes, I walk to the front of the room with my Dad's memory in my head and in my heart.

How many people have you not forgiven? How many grudges are you tightly holding on to? How many people do you refuse to call because of something silly that happened 17 years ago? The life meter is always ticking. Life is gone way too soon. Why is it so difficult to have a forgiving spirit?

It's so easy to stay angry. It's even easier to keep one's distance. We always think that there will be more time. "One day," "Some day," and "We'll see," turn into "I wish," "I should have," and "Why didn't I?"

Consider This: You can be a role model by teaching someone through your magnificence or through your miscues.

There's another piece to the Jim Smith Sr. story that relates to forgiveness. I had to check myself again, this time because of my friends' absence at the funeral. As I sat staring into the coffin, wiping away my tears, I thought about my father's past and our spotty relationship. From time to time, I looked into the crowd of supporters, searching for my family and my friends' comforting eyes. My family was there but, for a variety of reasons, many of my close friends were absent, save Paul Kallmeyer. Paul, one of my Titans, became one of my closest friends during our corporate days. He was also extremely helpful to me during my divorce. He became my confidant, my rock, and my means for just kicking back.

My emotions continued to get the best of me. The realization that my father was gone hurt immensely. "There was so much I could have done," I thought to myself. I was a mess. I remember Paul walking over to me some time during the viewing, bending over to kiss me on the cheek, and telling me that everything was going to be all right. Actually, I was surprised that he was there. I really did not expect him to make it. He had just found out about my father's death a couple of days before the funeral. Plus, he had to drive nearly two hours to get there from his home. My Dad's service was held in a neighborhood reminiscent of many depicted in movies portraying lower-class black urban life. Paul, who is white, really stood out. His being there will stay with me forever. To think that the only close friend of mine (my brother and I do have common friends who were in attendance) to attend would be my tall, white-lawyer, softball teammate, and friend was befuddling but memorable. I was thankful for the many cards and flowers I received, yet I wondered why more of my other close friends were not there.

Initially, I was disappointed by my friends' absence. Then I intentionally lost touch with many of them for awhile. My father's death, however, would help to create a valley of space in my heart for forgiveness. I let it go. Later, I never mentioned anything to any of them about how I felt. Why take them there again?

Today we get furious with people when they change their minds. We get violent when motorists cross in front of us on the highway. We become enraged when someone hangs up the phone on us. We go bonkers when shoppers have more than the required number of items in their shopping cart in the express lane. Where's our forgiving spirit? Why do we become so angry? Why do we take things so personally? Why not empower ourselves to become steadfast in the face of adversity?

I remember reading the following in the *Autobiography of Jackie Robinson: I Never Made It*:

I have memories. I remember standing alone at first base—the only black man on the field. I had to fight hard against loneliness, abuse, and the knowledge that any mistake I made would be magnified because I was the only black out there. I had to fight hard to become just another guy. I had to deny my true fighting spirit so that the noble experiment could succeed. When it finally did, I could

AWESOME
ADVICE

I've found that having a forgiving spirit has been significant in my life. When I've been in situations where I've needed to forgive, I remember that our essence—which is what spirit is—is that we are all loving people. My ability to let go, choose love, and move forward is a wonderful opportunity for me to connect with my core. These moments of forgiveness have changed who I am, what I believe, and how I interact with others. I hope that my actions will inspire others to have a more forgiving spirit.

—Janae Bower, Minneapolis

When I think of forgiveness, I immediately think of Anthony DeMello. In his book *The Way to Love*, he writes: "Every time you find yourself irritated or angry with someone, the one to look at is not that person but yourself. The question to ask is not 'What's wrong with this person?' but 'What does this irritation tell me about myself?' First look into the very real possibility that the reason why this person's defects or so-called defects annoy you is that you have them yourself. But you have repressed them and so are projecting them unconsciously into the other. . . . Another thing is also clear: You become irritated with this person because he/she is not living up to the expectations that have been programmed into you."

—Maria Garaitonandia, Cuernavaca, Mexico

become my own man; many people resented my impatience and honesty. But I never cared about acceptance as much as I cared about respect.

Jackie Robinson was the epitome of a forgiving spirit, and you can be, too. A forgiving spirit means:

- Refraining from thinking that it's always all about you (see chapter 17).
- Allowing room for others to make mistakes.
- "Being the change we wish to see in the world." —Mahatma Gandhi
- Owning your piece and not consistently holding others responsible for everything that's happened.
- Remembering that, as Samuel Johnson said, "great works are performed not by strength but by perseverance."

People who have moved from average to awesome have learned to forgive and move on.

Moving from Average to Awesome

This chapter is not only about forgiving. It's also about how you consistently have to look for ways to be the bigger person. This exercise will help you move from an average mindset to a more positive and powerful awesome way of living.

First, consider which statement describes how you think about creating win-win outcomes even you don't necessarily agree with what occurred:

- **Average:** You harbor resentment toward and disassociate yourself from those who disappoint you.
- **Awesome:** You're developing an incredible, forgiving spirit; not carrying personal disappointment and baggage around like a

bad habit. You're soliciting help from your Titans to help you unload your baggage. In your journal, you're writing about your forgiveness and action steps for mending fences.

Second, take some time and consider the questions below. Respond to the questions and be sure to explain your answers. Finally, rate yourself on your progress. If you are currently average, say so (A). If you feel you deserve an awesome rating, indicate that as well (AW). If you are neither average nor awesome but working toward being awesome, just write W.

Getting to Awesome

Key questions	Your response and explanation	Rating
When is it easy to forgive, and when is it not?		
Are you currently dealing with a situation that requires your forgiveness?		
When you forgive do, you also forget?		

Rate your progress: average (A), awesome (AW), or working toward awesome (W).

Chapter 16

Remember That the Cure for Your Pain Is in Your Pain

> There were times when my body was weak and not able to sustain me. I almost died and that's when I lost my fear of death and learned to live. I failed both personally and professionally, but I realized that I could persevere. There is nothing anyone can do to me that causes fear and that in turn allows me the freedom to do what I want to do.
>
> —ELIZABETH ANDREWS,
> CLINTON TOWNSHIP, MI

When I was a little boy, my father introduced me to the theory that "the cure for the pain is in the pain." To make sure that he had my full attention during our "character developmental" sessions, he used a black or brown leather belt as his visual aid. Before he commenced these lessons of "appropriate home and school comportment, responsibility, and discipline," he would passionately utter the phrase "this is going to hurt me more than it's going to hurt you." I did not believe him then, but I do now. Through my 46 years, I've learned some of my best lessons in life through pain—albeit emotional and psychological pain, *not physical pain.*

Why does emotional and psychological pain have to hurt so much? Why does it have to feel like our insides are being stretched from Connecticut to Cancún? Why does the pain have to linger like crumbs at the bottom of a toaster? Why does it have to prey on our minds incessantly? To remind us, to remind us, to remind us to *never again* do what caused it.

Pain has no prejudice and doesn't play favorites. All people experience hurt. Unfortunately, some people have to experience excruciating hurt and pain before they seek change.

Consider This: "Experience is a hard teacher because she gives the test first, the lesson afterwards." —Vernon Law

---

This is why some children have to touch the fire to understand that fire will burn you. It's why some students have to take a 1.0 grade-point average home with them after their first semester to understand that if they don't thoroughly apply themselves as college freshmen, they will invariably spend the next three and a half years playing catch-up—if they don't flunk out. It's why some employees have to get fired to realize that inappropriate workplace behavior will not be tolerated. It's why some people have to catch their best friends talking behind their backs before they reevaluate their friendships. Life teaches us a lesson every day.

Granted, some lessons are more painful than others, but the end result for many is that we focus on the pain rather than on the lesson and the action step we could take. And if the pain isn't intolerable, and we flunk the lesson, we usually venture right back into the same "pain game."

Our threshold for pain is unbelievable. That's why many of us stay in agonizing relationships and tormenting work situations. We hold on, hang on, latch on, and clasp on to whatever is causing our misery. One of my favorite inspirational stories is motivational speaker Les Brown's tale about the dog on the nail:

> A father walks his son to school every day. And every day they pass a dog that is lying on a porch. What makes this particular dog different than other dogs in the neighbor-hood is that this dog is yelping, groaning, crying—obviously in some pain.
>
> Well, father and son walk past the same dog on the same porch every day. Finally, one day, the little boy asks his father if he knows what's wrong with the dog. The father nods yes, saying that he has a pretty good idea what is causing the dog so much pain. He explains to his son that the dog is crying because he is lying on a nail. Stunned, the little boy asks his father why doesn't the dog just get up off the nail? The father replies that the nail must not hurt the dog enough yet.

Isn't that just like us? We moan, groan, cry, and complain to anyone in earshot. And if you're not in earshot, we email or text SMS you or call you on the phone. Some of us even develop a contingent of groupies and frequent criers who, without fail, show up to hear our monologues. If the price of admission were sound advice and resources, rather than BYOD (bring your own drama), attendance would quickly dwindle. Most times we exhaust more energy in talking about the pain than we do eliminating its source. For a litany of reasons, including fear, timing, guilt, and a lack of courage, we don't get off of our nails. As students of life, we fail

AWESOME
ADVICE

On the outside, people in my life saw me as a confident, talented winner, the kind of person who was good at everything she tried: school, sports, various jobs. They didn't see that on the inside, I was slowly becoming more and more obsessed with perfection; I was driven by a fear I couldn't name. I felt like everything out of my mouth was an excuse. If something went wrong, I could not admit to a mistake. I had to collect the evidence of perfection, but I didn't know what I was trying to prove. I felt like I was on trial for my life, but I didn't know why.

The fear and stress of perfectionism drove me to the edge of the cliff, and I finally let someone see my pain. She asked me, "What's the worst thing that could happen if you make a mistake?" I realized that in my heart I believed that if I were wrong, I would be seen as a bad person. That would break my heart, and I just couldn't bear it. I had to let go. It wasn't that I changed my mind; my mind was changed.

Afterward, when I made a mistake, I learned to admit it and saw that the world did not crumble as a result. In fact, I've come to believe that mistakes are the building blocks of excellence, allowing the mind and body to find the best approach by eliminating the ones that don't work. All those years I had been robbing myself of the very thing that would really move me toward my full potential. Today, perfection isn't good enough for me.

—Shannon Percy, Minneapolis

to take copious notes about the painful lessons we're being taught, and we don't move on.

If we sit up straight, clear our minds, and pay close attention to what's going on around us, we can learn plenty about ourselves and about others. We can learn from the broken promises, the divorces, the firings, the punishments, the disappointments, the bankruptcies, the promotion denials, the ruined friendships, and the runner-up finishes. Through these trials, we can learn to stop putting ourselves in certain situations, hopefully mustering the much-needed strength to incorporate into our lives the four Cs of change: commitment, consistency, courage, and confidence.

We can learn who brings out our Dr. Jekyll and who brings out our Mr. or Mrs. Hyde. We can learn to love ourselves so much that we will *stop* starring in reruns of those morbid shows, stop repeating patterns of pain.

Some pain, however, a different kind of pain, catches us off guard. Life doesn't always provide planning and preparation for pain. Life isn't fair that way. And for two of my friends, a type of pain over which they had no control slid in totally unexpectedly 10 years ago, changing their lives forever.

Bill and Lynne Hart both had prosperous careers and "on the side" hobby/business pursuits to stay busy, happy, centered, and connected to the community. They also had a growing, positive, always-smiling, and ambitious teenager, Kelby.

Bill arrived home one evening and made a beeline to the backyard to get the dog and take him on their daily pre-evening, clear-your-mind, man-and-his-dog walk. Lynne was in the kitchen preparing dinner, and Kelby was upstairs completing his homework.

Returning from the walk, Bill, put the dog back in the yard and called for Kelby to come down and fill him in on his school day. Wearing only his blue and gold University of Michigan basketball trunks and sneakers, Kelby raced down the stairs to greet his father.

Since Bill knew that Kelby had taken his preseason physical for football that day, he quickly cut to the results after small talk about school. Kelby said that he had failed the physical because his knee was still banged up from a previous fall. However, the spirited 14-year-old said, loud enough so that his mother could hear him in the kitchen, "That's OK. I'm still 5 feet, 5 and a half inches, and 125 pounds!" I'm taller than you, Mom!" Bill smiled, looked at his son, and began to talk about getting his knee looked at so that he could join the team soon.

Before Bill finished his next sentence, Kelby fell back on the floor, unconscious. Bill yelled for Lynne to come into the room! She called the ambulance as he frantically tried to bring Kelby to. Desperately, Bill attempted mouth-to-mouth resuscitation and CPR, but to no avail. The ambulance arrived and Kelby was whisked to the hospital.

A few hours later, Kelby died of natural causes. Fourteen years old, 5 feet, 5 and a half inches, 125 pounds. It was going to be difficult for Bill and Lynne to find the cure for their pain in this pain.

I went to visit them recently to interview them for this book. When Bill met me at the door, his face and a comment under his breath signaled that he had forgotten about our meeting. He had made other plans. I told him that we could reschedule and that I would come back another time. But he insisted that I come in and at least get a tour of the house. I greeted Lynne with a warm hug, and then Bill turned into Julie McCoy (that is, the star of TV's *The Love Boat*), giving me my tour of the "Hart estate."

From bathrooms to bedrooms, sitting rooms to antique rooms, reflection rooms to eating rooms, I saw everything, save Kelby's room. Pointing to the white, closed door, Bill showed me where Kelby's room (still exactly the way Kelby had left it) was, but we did not go in. We had stopped in Bill's third-floor memora-bilia room, a shrine to Muhammad Ali and vintage jazz, when he began to talk about Kelby. He started by sharing how Kelby used to sneak into their bedroom in the morning to get Bill's cologne to wear. Bill laughed, as he told the story, adding that he had gone into Kelby's room that morning to put on his son's prized CK cologne.

Laughter turned to tears as Bill recounted the story to me, moment by moment, second by second. He squeezed his work tie in his hand as if he were holding Kelby's hand for the last time. My powerful friend missed his son dearly. He said that he and Lynne now take one day at a time, that some days are harder than others. They keep reminding themselves that "it is what it is and it can be no other way."

I was paralyzed. Bill was in tears. I kept thinking about Kelby's last words, "I'm 5 feet, 5 and a half inches, 125 pounds!"

Honoring his time and wanting to make the tears go away, I said to Bill that he better get ready to head out. We hugged and returned downstairs. I said goodbye to Lynne, thanking her for permitting me to share Kelby with them. Within seconds, as she thought about her departed angel, she began to cry. "We're dealing with it, Jim. . . . He was such a sweet kid. . . . I miss my baby," she said as I headed to the front door. I drove home pondering the life-altering journey I had been on ever since I started writing this book.

Bill and Lynne smile a lot these days. They are best friends. Their relationship is fabulous. They provide a consistent supply of love and support for each other. Kelby's memory will forever be in their souls. His pictures are in every room. But knowing Bill as I do, I know Kelby's memory fuels his drive to create awesome lives for those he touches. As both Bill and Lynne will tell you, "It is what it is and it can be no other way."

Bill and Lynne have found a way to deal with their pain. However, the pain from such a tragedy, and the kind of lessons

AWESOME
ADVICE

I am learning to "be" with whatever is happening in my life—good and not so good. To feel pain is as human as feeling joy—to feel anger is as essential as feeling compassion. To avoid any emotion is to omit an essential piece in the mosaic of life.

We did indeed learn these same lessons as children learning to cross the street: stop, look, and listen. . . .

—Judy Chapman, Toronto

learned, are quite different from the pain and lessons from broken promises, divorces, firings, and the like, situations to which we contribute (to a greater or lesser extent) and that we can learn to avoid. However, there's a blessin' in every lesson.

Awesome people have accumulated, and have learned from, myriad life lessons. They do see the blessin'. Through these lessons, they've learned to toughen their resolve. Some lessons were pleasurable, but others were excruciatingly painful. Pay attention, and listen closely: Sometimes the cure for the pain is in the pain.

Moving from Average to Awesome

This chapter is not only about overcoming painful moments. It's also about how you can learn and grow from your experiences and mistakes. This exercise will help you move from an average mindset to a more positive and powerful awesome way of living.

First, consider which statement describes how you think about what experiences teach you:

- **Average:** You find yourself in the same or similar painful situations over and over again.
- **Awesome:** You're learning from the painful situations that come your way and applying these lessons to create powerful, positive differences in your life. You are resolving, then putting into motion, behavior changes that suggest that you will not dive into your pain again—no matter how tempting it may be.

Second, take some time and consider the questions below. Respond to the questions and be sure to explain your answers. Finally, rate yourself on your progress. If you are currently average, say so (A). If you feel you deserve an awesome rating, indicate that as well (AW). If you are neither average nor awesome but working toward being awesome, just write W.

Getting to Awesome

Key questions	Your response and explanation	Rating
What did you learn from your last painful experience? How have you incorporated that lesson into your life?		
What painful experience are you still having a difficult time shaking off?		
Based on feedback you've received from others, what situations should you avoid to become more effective in your professional and personal life?		

Rate your progress: average (A), awesome (AW), or working toward awesome (W).

Chapter 17

Look for Opportunities to Elevate Others

> What "gets me up" is my dedication to help others discover more of who they are. Helping others connect what they believe to what they say and do is my motivator.
>
> —RENEE GALLART, NEW HOPE, PA

The clock—tick, tick, tick—was winding down to the finish. Less than four minutes remained in the game. Mr. Momentum had changed sidelines and was now proudly wearing Widener blue and yellow. My teammates and I were eagerly and confidently inching closer to winning the 1981 Division III National Football Championship in the Amos Alonzo Stagg Bowl. The Dayton Flyers were scrambling to regain the lead they had held so comfortably for three-and-a-half quarters.

Dayton had the ball on its own 35-yard line, but we had the lead, 14–10. It was an ironic scenario, promising to provide some poetic justice, for this was the long-anticipated rematch of the previous year's semifinal thriller, which Dayton had convincingly won 28–24, overcoming a 24–0 halftime deficit. They won the national championship in their next game, while we soaked our injuries and made excuses for what could have and should have happened.

I played right defensive cornerback. I looked over to their sideline before going to our huddle to see if I could determine what play they were going to run next. With my eyes fixed on their coach, I attempted to read his lips. Mission accomplished. The receiver was going to run about 10 yards, stop, fake right, then turn left, looking to catch the pass that should already be in flight. Dayton was going to run the play right in my direction! I was so confident that I knew what was coming, I never did report to our makeshift huddle to hear the defensive call. Actually, this was my déjà vu. I had seen this entire scenario in my head the previous night.

My mind raced as I waited during those precious few seconds before the play unfolded. I determined that I would make the interception and race the 45 or so yards down the field untouched for the touchdown.

Once in the end zone, I would first take off my helmet and graciously smile for the camera; then say "hi" to my mother, Rodney, and other family members; then do some sort of commemorative dance reminiscent of the Soul Train *dancers; and finally jump into the arms of my jubilant teammates, who would join me, within seconds, in my jubilant end zone celebration.*

I was Walter Mitty in a football uniform.

I did have the play called right. The receiver ran about eight yards in my direction, but he failed to fake, heading directly to the sideline to make the reception and get out of bounds. This was even better than I had dreamed. "Professional football and highlight reel here I come," I thought as I moved to catch the brown leather spiral heading in my direction. I ran and then leaped for the ball as it headed directly toward my outstretched arms. For a fraction of a second, I took my eyes off it to see if my path to a national championship ring, the cover of *Sports Illustrated*, and an end zone celebration was still clear. I saw nothing but pristine green grass. When I looked up again, I watched the ball sail through my fingers.

I dropped the ball!

I dropped the ball!

I dropped the ball!

Widener won the game 17–10. I did receive my national championship ring. But more than that, I learned a couple of lessons: First, it's not always all about me. Second, not everything is always going to go as planned, but it can still work incredibly well.

Earlier in the game, I had made the key block that enabled our punt returner, Tom Deery, to race 76 yards for our first touchdown and begin our comeback. It was a significant contribution to our winning the game, but not the way I had envisioned making the highlight reel. I wanted to score the winning touchdown. I wanted to make *the* big play. I wanted to be on *The Tonight Show*. I wanted to be the star of the game. I wanted the reporters around my locker after the game. I wanted to get to the team bus late because autograph seekers were hounding me like paparazzi at a Britney Spears sighting.

Don't be misled; I was ecstatic that we won. We finished the season 13–0. In silent prayer, I thanked God and briefly reflected on our accomplishment, then jumped on the pile of giddy Widener football players celebrating in the middle of the field. Nevertheless, while flying back to campus that evening, I looked out the airplane window, staring, searching into the darkness. While my teammates made enough noise to conjure up thoughts of every January 1 at midnight, I tried to figure out how and why I had dropped that pass.

I wanted my championship game experience to be special, like so many other memories in my sports past. I always scored the winning basket or got the key hit. I wanted more than to simply play in the game or make a key block, which to my mind were like making the lemonade or bringing the charcoal to the family reunion: important—maybe even essential—but not at all glamorous or noteworthy. I wanted the Oscar for best leading man in a national championship college football game, not best supporting actor.

Consider This: "He who wants a place in the sun should expect blisters."
—Author unknown

Fast forward to now. That lesson from college football is etched in my mind. You can play a powerful role in any endeavor without always having to be the star. (Still, if I had a chance to do it all over again, I would have caught the interception, scored the touchdown, and hoped that life would serve up another opportunity for me to learn that awesome lesson. Just kidding . . . I think.)

Playing Robin to someone else's Batman is not the easiest occupation, especially when Batman doesn't send any credit your way. Haven't you seen entertainers fighting over the microphone to determine who was going to sing or talk? In the corporate training arena, I've seen professional trainers have egotistical moments, quarreling before, during, and after sessions over who was going to facilitate the perceived most prominent segments of the workshop. I've seen speakers go way over their allotted presentation time because they reeked of "it's all about me."

Realizing that it's not always about you means being humble, self-sacrificing, confident, intuitive, and gracious. Occasionally, we need to be the learner, the listener, the student, the chorus—

the Pips to Gladys Knight, the Black-Eyed Peas to Fergie. There's so much we can gain by moving away from center stage.

I worked with one of my favorite clients not too long ago. My deliverables included facilitating a diversity train-the-trainer session on Wednesday and Thursday, then leading a half-day diversity session on the subsequent Tuesday morning. I usually fly home immediately after my work is completed, but this time, because I would be returning to the same client site in Chicago in a few days, I decided to stay over the weekend. That way I could save my client money by eliminating a round-trip airfare; in addition, I wanted uninterrupted quiet time to work on this book. The initial manuscript was nearly complete, and having Friday, Saturday, Sunday, and Monday to apply the finishing touches seemed very appealing. I conjured up memories of completing my final thesis for my graduate school project at Temple. I took a week off from work and lived in the library. I read and typed, read and typed, until my 90-page, single-spaced project was finished. Similarly, meals aside, I planned to stay in my hotel room until the manuscript was done!

Before I left the building on Thursday, however, my client, Tony Graham, asked me if I had any plans for Friday. I told him of my intention to go into seclusion with my manuscript and he laughed. He then dangled the big, fat, juicy carrot, the excuse that would alter my plans and provide another anecdote for this book. He said that the company was bringing in motivational speaker Les Brown to keynote at their national sales meeting in July. He said that he was going to watch Les give a motivational talk to a group of educators, then take him to lunch to discuss the July engagement. Then he dangled the carrot lower, right in my salivating face. He asked if I would like to join him. After taking a full thousandth of a second to think it over, I asked Tony what time he would be by in the morning to pick me up. He could have said 3:00 a.m. and I still would have been ready.

With regard to motivational speaking, I've admired Les's work for over 20 years. He was the measuring stick I used for other speakers, including myself. I'd seen Les speak numerous times, could recount many of his powerful stories and quotes, and had bought his tapes and read his books. But I'd never been up close and personal with him.

I went to bed that night thinking, "I'm going to meet Les Brown, I'm going to meet Les Brown. He could certainly give my career a boost, assist with my book and my speaking." I dreamed of what gifts the next day would provide. I was going to meet the Michael Jordan, the Bette Davis, the Frank Sinatra, the Jesse Owens, the Josephine Baker, the Beethoven, the Picasso of motivational speaking. I wouldn't need to have the hotel call and wake me up in the morning. This career- and life-changing opportunity would be my wake-up call. I was meeting *the* Motivator, the man who had taught me, albeit from a distance, the most about the rhythm, pace, movement, voice quality, and other mechanics of motivational speaking.

Tony arrived at 6:00 a.m. We drove 90 minutes to the school auditorium to watch Les do his thing. After nearly two hours of vintage Les, the attendees were ready to take on the world and I was ready to take Les to lunch.

Les joined us, and the three of us drove to the restaurant. With Tony behind the wheel and me behind Les in the passenger seat, I prepped to blitzkrieg Les with the 5,322 questions I'd waited nearly 20 years to ask. Then it hit me. This wasn't about me! This was about Tony, my client, securing Les Brown to speak at his key sales meeting. This was his meeting. Tony needed all the precious time we had to question and connect with his speaker. As much as I wanted to take the microphone, I relented; I would sit on the bench during this game. In the car and during lunch, I listened, listened, and listened, save for one brief moment in the car when Tony pulled over to ask for directions and Les asked me what was my claim to fame. In 30 seconds, I gave him a wow that I'm sure would have made Lisa Nichols very proud (turn back to the introduction to find out what a wow is).

After his business conversation with Tony was over, Les turned the conversation to me. Taking advantage of my brief moment (my time was limited because Les's limousine was waiting out front to drive him to the airport), I was extremely intentional. I candidly and passionately shared my past but mostly my future, focusing primarily on this book and my motivational speaking pursuits. He listened intently, smiling, taking it all in. I could see his mind working. I sensed that we connected. He said I had a gift, that there was something special about me. With that, he gave me his home phone number, asked if he could write the foreword for the book you're now reading, and headed to the car. Partially stunned, I stopped him to see if he was serious or if I was just hearing things. He did not blink, saying he would be honored. What a moment!

I learned plenty just by watching and listening to him during his conversation with Tony, a virtual needs-assessment meeting. My mind took thorough notes. I learned more by merely listening than I ever would have if I had run my mouth or competed with Tony for airtime.

As we drove back to my hotel, Tony thanked me for not interrupting him while he took care of his business. He said he really appreciated that I put my enthusiasm and my agenda on hold. I told him that I had learned a long time ago that it is not always about me.

A key ingredient in being awesome is realizing that it's not always about you. One way you can demonstrate this is by helping other people become awesome. Tony's meeting conversation was more significant than my groupie adulations. Les and Tony had to connect for Les to have a successful keynote in July.

Freely give your time, resources, and support to people who could benefit from your talents, wisdom, and skills. My job has put

AWESOME ADVICE

The following article was written by Elmer Smith for the Philadelphia Daily News *after the 2002 Academy Awards. The article discusses the epitome of selflessness. Read how some special actors demonstrated, through their giving, that it's not always all about them.*

I didn't see Ossie Davis or Ruby Dee when the cameras scanned that glittering crowd at the Oscar ceremonies Sunday. Maybe I missed them. They aren't the kind who stand out in a 24-carat crowd. But I could feel them Sunday as Sidney Poitier, Denzel Washington and Halle Berry took turns accepting the accolades of their peers. I could feel Paul Robeson, Oscar Michaux, Hattie McDaniels.

And Steppin Fetchit.

"He was one of my heroes," Ossie Davis told me once, on a night I will never forget . . . a night that helped create a story about our responsibility to hold open those doors that someone held open or kicked down for us in whatever fields we labor in.

Denzel Washington and Halle Berry received the recognition that they earned through their own hard work and artistry. Nobody gave them anything. But they understood that they had crossed a bridge built by people who came before them and that it doesn't take anything from them to acknowledge that. That's why Denzel remembered Sidney Poitier and Halle Berry remembered Spike Lee. And that's why Ossie Davis remembered Steppin Fetchit on a night when my wife and I fawned over him and Ruby Dee.

This was nine years ago at the home of (friends) Larry and Larverne Depte . . . [who had developed a professional and personal relationship with the two movie greats]. My wife and I jumped at the chance when the Deptes asked if we'd like to meet Ossie and Ruby at a small dinner party at the Deptes' home.

We talked about marriage—they had been married for 45 years at the time—and about the civil rights movement, and their meetings with Malcolm X and Martin Luther King Jr. When we finally steered the conversation around to their acting careers, I told them how much I admired them for refusing roles that would demean them or us. They shrugged it off. When I persisted, he told me why Steppin Fetchit was such an important pioneer.

Fetchit had made a career out of playing the foot-shuffling, head-scratching stereotype. Watching it used to make me cringe. I had always felt he sold us all out to get rich. Ossie Davis and Ruby Davis corrected me. He did what he had to do to get his foot in the door, Davis told me. And when he did, he held the door open for others like them. He knew exactly what he was doing and why he had to do it, Davis said. Steppin Fetchit shuffled his feet and scratched his head so we would only have to shuffle our feet, Davis said.

By the time we came along, Ruby Dee said, we could say, "OK, boss, I don't mind shuffling, but I won't scratch my head."

The black actors who followed them didn't have to shuffle or scratch their heads because someone else had already paid that price. It was paid by Oscar Michaux, a brilliant black filmmaker who had to accept the demeaning roles that were a black actor's staple so he could raise the money to make films that portrayed black families and individuals in ways that most America wasn't used to seeing us in.

Paul Robeson used to look so natural in bib-top overalls with a shovel in his hand that you could almost forget that he was a brilliant scholar who had earned a Phi Beta Kappa key at Rutgers University. There were others whose names wouldn't mean very much to you and me. I'm sorry I can't remember their contributions.

But they will never be forgotten—as long as people like Ossie and Ruby and Denzel and Halle can keep a foot in the door.

—Reprinted with permission from the
Philadelphia Daily News, March 27, 2002

me in a position to meet thousands of people. Many are craving for a timely word, a pat on the back, a vote of confidence, or just a second of my time. You can become someone's Titan by volunteering your time or your energy, and by moving that spotlight in his or her direction. And if you really want to grow, then seek out opportunities to give, coach, mentor, or assist people who are different from you. There are many in your professional and personal life who can benefit from your special skills, experiences, and talents.

You have an awful lot to offer even if you have more yesterdays than tomorrows. We grow from our responses to people, projects, challenges, and champions.

Treat every day like you have not done your best work yet.

I am who I am largely because people saw something in me and decided to help fine-tune it, shape it, and help others to benefit from it. Now I do the same and you can, too. But to do so you have to remember that it's not always all about you.

Moving from Average to Awesome

This chapter is not only about helping others become awesome. It's also about how you can learn, grow, and prosper from being in a support role. This exercise will help you move from an average mindset to a more positive and powerful awesome way of living.

First, consider which statement describes how you think about always getting top billing:

- **Average:** You focus solely on your own agenda—what's in it for you. You're always looking for opportunities to grab the spotlight or attention for yourself.
- **Awesome:** You routinely look for opportunities to help others become awesome. As a trainer or speaking professional, you know that the most important people in the room are the ones

sitting in front of you. You share your skills, trade secrets, and network of colleagues and friends. You're truly OK with not always having to be behind the steering wheel, and you actually seek opportunities to steer the conversation someone else's way and take direction from him or her.

Second, take some time and consider the questions below. Respond to the questions and be sure to explain your answers. Finally, rate yourself on your progress. If you are currently average, say so (A). If you feel you deserve an awesome rating, indicate that as well (AW). If you are neither average nor awesome but working toward being awesome, just write W.

Getting to Awesome

Key questions	Your response and explanation	Rating
In what situations do you get agitated or annoyed when your idea or recommendation is not selected?		
Do you always have to have the last word or final say?		
What gets in the way of you playing a more supportive role more often?		

Rate your progress: average (A), awesome (AW), or working toward awesome (W).

Chapter 18

Fearlessly Unleash Your Greatness and Creativity

> Living the transformational life for the past eight months or so has been such a gift. Some call it the midlife crisis. We can get so caught up in what others think of us—where we are personally and professionally. I call it transformation time, and I love it. I'm moving! I'm growing! I'm dancing! It's so rewarding. I'm no longer looking for approval. Words cannot even describe the power.
>
> —RAJEAN BIFANO, FLAGSTAFF, AZ

Been to a wedding lately? Beautiful wedding party? How was the reception? Great food? How was the music? Did *that* person show up? Which person, you ask? You know who I'm referring to—that "Gene, Gene, the Dancing Machine" person. He or she is that special, happy, outgoing, extroverted person who commandeers the dance floor. Others at the reception point and laugh at him or her, thinking that he or she is more inspired by adult beverage consumption than by the tunes emanating from the deejay's speakers.

But they're wrong; this person caught dance fever by simply deciding that he or she was going to have an awesome time. First it's the Electric Slide, then the Cha Cha Slide, the Macarena, and the Twist. After the Chicken Dance, Shout, the YMCA, and the Soul Train Line, you can tell that he or she is just warming up. As you watch him or her in the conga line, you can tell that he or she is in the *zone*, the dance trance, the party hearty pavilion. And guess what? He or she doesn't care who's watching.

Former baseball pitching great Satchel Paige provided one of my all-time favorite quotes when he described how he believed we should live our life: "Dream like you will live forever, work like you don't need the money, love like you have never been hurt, and dance like nobody's watching!"

Wow! What would happen if you could transfer this way of thinking to everything you do? What would happen if you lived as if nobody was watching, unconcerned about

- consistently trying to please people
- always asking for permission to do the simplest things
- what management will say
- wearing clothes that are in line with what others will be wearing
- doing things the way they've always been done
- whether your professor or teacher will grade you more for quantity than for creativity
- how others receive your passion for . . .
- how long it will take you to . . .
- what others think about your potential or ability
- being the first to start dancing at the party

- doing everything exactly the "right way"
- whether you're following the exact steps others took to reach a goal.

Can you imagine being like this? We can be so driven by and so wedded to what others say and what others think that we don't let our genius, our creativity, our spontaneity, or our true colors come out to play.

Consider This: It is far better to be free to govern, or misgovern, yourself than to be governed by anybody else.
—Kwame Nkrumah

Our lives are so inundated with organizational and societal mores and norms that we seldom unleash our greatness, our power, and our gifts. This is not a rallying cry for being self-centered and selfish. Nor is it a call for reckless behavior. It's a cheer for being unique, being spontaneous, being in the moment, hearing the beat, then going for it without trepidation and regret.

Those times when you do let your hair down, don't you usually say at some point, "All right, that was fun! I need to do this more often." That's what I'm suggesting: Do "it" more often. Soon "it" will become a part of you.

I started dancing like no one was watching in the 1960s, when I would perform concerts in my bedroom with my brothers Jackie, Tito, Marlon, Jermaine, and Michael. Yes, I was the sixth member of the fabulous Jackson 5 before Randy arrived on the scene. I'd play one of our many albums, position my GI Joes as audience members, put on one of my mother's huge Afro wigs, move my dresser mirror closer, and dance and sing for hours. I knew every word to every song. Those moments have certainly played a role in shaping my creativity, my speaking, my training style, and my free spirit.

How many people do you know who are so predictable they're boring? How many people do you know who don't get excited about anything, preferring to remain in a place of calm and casual reserve? Les Brown says that if you live your life being casual, you'll become a casualty.

We become settlers. We settle for dead-end jobs. We settle for living in neighborhoods that drive us up the wall. We settle for relationships from which we don't grow. We learn to accept the circumstances we've been given. As a result, because we're afraid to take risks and we fear failure, driven by what others are going to say about what we do and how we do it, we live like somebody's watching all the time. We don't hear the dance music.

Consider This: "The impulse to dream had been slowly beaten out of me by experience. Now it surged up again and I hungered for books, new ways of looking and seeing." —Richard Wright

It's as if we constantly need approval to flourish.

I rely heavily on the customer service I receive, especially considering my heavy travel schedule. If I had a brick for every person who has said to me, "Wait a second, I have to ask my manager if I could do that," or "That's not my job. I'm only the . . . ," I would be able to build skyscrapers in all 50 states and have enough bricks remaining to build a barbeque pit in every backyard in Philadelphia. And my requests are not that cumbersome. Can I have an extra one of those? Please remove this from my bill because I did not order that. Can you switch my room because this one has . . . ?

It's not until I drop the name of the company I'm representing that they jump. This gets tiresome fast.

It doesn't take a brain surgeon to determine that there are more people who don't dance like nobody's watching than those who do. Add to that the number of people who live their lives playing to keep the score close rather than to win and you have a Grand Canyon of unfulfilled people. This phenomenon manifests itself in many ways.

Certain ethnic groups, at times, seek safe careers historically germane to their culture because they think it's the appropriate, acceptable, or the preferred thing to do. Here come the generalizations: Indian, medicine; Jewish, law protection; Irish, law enforcement. Some people are more driven by obtaining titles and labels (manager, vice president, doctor, esquire, supervisor, head this, head that) than obtaining happiness. Start setting and clearing your own personal achievement bar and stop worrying about what other people say or think. Put your energy where your dreams are (and don't put your dreams on layaway).

Doing just that is how

- Jim Hensen gave us the muppets.
- Dick Vitale gives us "Awesome Baby!"
- Wilma Rudolph and Flo Jo gave us Olympic records and gold medals.
- Flip Wilson gave us Geraldine.
- Zany Dennis Rodman turned a mediocre basketball career into million-dollar contracts, movies, wrestling matches, a best-selling book, and five NBA championship rings.
- Carol Burnett, Chris Rock, Bill Cosby, Robin Williams, and Whoopi Goldberg have made us laugh for years with their special brand of comedy.
- Barack Obama courageously ignored the naysayers during his presidential run.

AWESOME ADVICE

You have to make it happen for yourself because nobody else will do it for you. You have to do what your heart tells you to. But that's a lot easier said than done.

After working as a manufacturer's sales representative selling wholesale to gift shops for about a year and making very little money (depending on the season), I knew I couldn't do this job forever. I needed something more challenging and with more stability. I had been floating from one job to the next for four years.

After some long thought, I considered some sort of job working with children. At every party, I ended up playing with the kids or just talking to them. I often found children more stimulating and interesting than adults. I decided that before I made another job change, I would take a graduate school course in education. I was quite hooked on the idea of working with children, regardless of what others thought.

My next dilemma was that I was 27, without any formal or practical training in education. How could I get a job teaching, even with a graduate degree in another subject area (I was finishing up my MBA), without any experience in the field of education?

One day, after a *horrible* sales call, I drove from Cape May [NJ] to Blue Bell [PA] for a potential new account. Not only didn't they buy anything, I got a speeding ticket!

I then drove by a school. I circled the school twice, wanting to go in and inquire about teaching opportunities, but I started thinking about not having a degree in education. Nevertheless, I finally pulled into the school parking lot and went in. I at least looked like I was ready for an interview, dressed in a sharp business suit, carrying a briefcase. I asked one of the office staff to see the principal, but she just gave me the hairy eyeball and looked me up and down before answering. I explained to her that I was a grad student at Cabrini College and was interested in volunteering or obtaining information about a part-time job.

Suddenly the principal popped up from behind the file cabinet with a guilty grin. He explained that it was common for parents to arrive this week, before school starts, to complain about their children's placement with a teacher. He thought that I was a bullet he should dodge. As fate would have it, he was also an adjunct professor at Cabrini and arranged for me to get an interview for a lunch aide job. I took the job on the remote chance I'd get an additional three-hours-a-day classroom aide job that, combined, would pay enough to help with my mortgage and some of my student loans.

Because of my dream to work with children, and by taking a risk to make it happen, and by not letting others' opinions become my reality, I ended up working at the same school throughout grad school as an aide. When I graduated, I got a long-term substitute spot for a year, and then I got a contract for a permanent position. I've been feeling awesome ever since! I love being with children! And I don't care that it's not the perceived awesome sales job that others think I should have.

—Danielle Kallmeyer, Montgomeryville, PA

If you make public or work-related presentations, stretch yourself. Dare to be different. There's too much DBPP (death by PowerPoint). Begin your presentation from the back of the room. Stand on a chair if it enhances your message and others' viewership. Raise your voice if it better gets your message across. Start your session with an activity rather than introducing the objectives first. Use more visuals—most people think in pictures rather than words anyway.

Be a walking, talking visual aid for living your dreams and for dancing like nobody's watching. You don't get in life what you want; you get what you are and what you expect!

Oh, one more thing: Stop laughing at the person dancing at the wedding reception. Get up and join him or her! Now slide to the left. Slide to the right. Jump two times. Now give me some cha cha! You got it!

Moving from Average to Awesome

This chapter is not only about living life on your own terms. It's also about how you can stretch and push your talents to groundbreaking territories. This exercise will help you move from an average mindset to a more positive and powerful awesome way of living.

First, consider which statement describes how you think about dancing like nobody's watching:

- **Average:** You settle for being just OK. You wait for opportunities to knock on your door. Through your behavior, you seemingly ask for approval and permission to live or to perform your job. You're consumed with what others think of you.
- **Awesome:** You fearlessly unleash your greatness and creativity. You take risks and learn from them. You stretch yourself to be awesome, outstanding, and happy. You get on the dance floor first. You're always looking for fresh, new approaches. You're living your dreams.

Second, take some time and consider the questions below. Respond to the questions and be sure to explain your answers. Finally, rate yourself on your progress. If you are currently average, say so (A). If you feel you deserve an awesome rating, indicate that as well (AW). If you are neither average nor awesome but working toward being awesome, just write W.

Getting to Awesome

Key questions	Your response and explanation	Rating
Do you overreact to constructive feedback?		
When are you apprehensive about trying something that has never been attempted before?		
How do you adjust your mindset to deal with individuals who have a "dance like everybody's watching" spirit?		

Rate your progress: average (A), awesome (AW), or working toward awesome (W).

Chapter 19

Listen to the Music, Then Produce Awesome Results

When things go wrong, don't go with them.

—LES BROWN, POTOMAC, MD

I've referred to movies several times in this book. Something happens during most movies to foreshadow or hint at what's going to occur next. Think about it. What happens during a movie that suggests something good, tragic, triumphant, grand, exhilarating, sad, or momentous is going to happen? If you're thinking music, you're right. Whether it's fast, loud, up-tempo, inspirational, dramatic, slow, or lovey-dovey, you can get a sense of what's about to occur from the music. The same thing happens in life.

We hear but we don't always listen to the music.

I used to work for a major bank in Philadelphia. One reason I took the job was because it was my first opportunity to work in

197

the city. This job helped move me closer to my roots, my Mom (who worked across the street), my brother (who worked three blocks away), and my home. I was there for several months before I started to hear the music.

Mergers and acquisitions were being mentioned in the newspaper every day. Some huge company was always gobbling up some other smaller company. Or two powerhouses were joining forces to become Godzilla Goliath Sr. And various banks, including my company, were always being mentioned.

The highest-ranking female executive, a person loved and admired by numerous people in the bank, left the organization. When she acknowledged that she was leaving to pursue other personal interests, I heard the music become louder.

The rumors in the banking industry that we were in play—meaning that other banks were considering acquiring us—wouldn't go away. The music got louder.

Consider This: "Wisdom is knowing less but understanding more." —Author unknown

Other key management members left for "other opportunities." It was hard to hear myself think over the music.

The bank's CEO put an ad in the Sunday newspaper saying we would not be acquired. For me, that put the music at a fever pitch. Two weeks later, we were sold. The music was deafening!

My greatest surprise was that nearly everyone else seemed surprised. People were bewildered, distraught, angry, and bitter. The timing, I'm sure, had something to do with their reactions. We were acquired several weeks before Thanksgiving. But I was blown away that so many people reacted as though they did not have a clue. I had heard the music—why hadn't they?

Why is it that we so often don't hear the music? Or maybe the question should be: Why don't we react when we hear the music?

The music we hear can be our hearts, our mind, or our subconscious, saying "Don't do it" or "Move on" or "You've had enough" or "You're going to get hurt." Your music can be your spouse saying "You don't listen to me," "You don't give me any affection anymore," "We don't do the things we used to do," and ultimately "You don't love me anymore." Your music could be your boss saying, "We're going to give the special project to someone else; hang in there, and we'll be looking at you the next time." Your music could be the silent treatment you now receive from the person who used to shower you with love letters, sweet conversation, lengthy phone calls, timely emails, and cards of endearment. Your music could be your body grumbling that it's time for a checkup. Your music could be the vibes you intuitively feel right before you get the phone call from the friend you haven't spoken to in years.

Some people call it vibes, their gut, or their intuition. I call it music.

My father did not listen to the music before we moved away. My friend Leah did not listen to the music when her husband sent her all kinds of lyrics of frustration, indicating he was ready to end their relationship. The music began to hurt her ears though, when, out of the blue, he called to say he wasn't coming back home and that there was nothing she could say or do to change his mind.

At times, when we hear the music, we ignore it, avoid it, or turn it down. However, when we enjoy the beat, we turn the music up. We blast it.

You see it when sports teams and athletes make incredible comebacks after seemingly being down and out. You see it when people make monumental shifts to right their lives, professional or personal. You see it when singers and speakers get on a roll in front of audiences. They start singing songs and sharing anecdotes that weren't in the practice routine.

AWESOME
ADVICE

I find it very sad to hear about people who go all of their lives searching for the "true meaning of life" as if it is a tangible thing that is hidden in some secret, magical place. I believe that the true meaning of life is something that we must create for ourselves. Just as I choose to create an awesome rather than average life for myself, I can also create an awesome meaning for my life.

For me the meaning of my life is in being in love with life every day and keeping my eyes open to everything it has to offer. Whether it's being in love with someone or something or a special place or time, within that love I acquire the unique kind of passion required for an awesome life. This kind of passion provides me with the courage and the energy to do awesome things, to have awesome relationships, and to be an awesome individual. My eyes and heart are open to experiences every day that create that feeling of love and passion. I want to be carried away by it. The most important thing I try to remember is this:

The music of life is around us every day. You can either choose to dance to it or you can lose yourself in it. Lose yourself in the music and if you do, life, your life, will be awesome!

—Lisa Dommer, Columbus

Sonny Elia taught and coached in the Philadelphia school system for 24 years. He became one of my Titans/Dads when I was in the ninth grade. He coached my junior varsity baseball and basketball teams. During the summer months, I went to his Mr. Basketball Camp, first as a camper and then as a counselor. Today the camp is the official Philadelphia 76ers basketball camp.

Sonny's music started when teaching stopped being fun, when what once had been a passion evolved into a frustrating job. The music also took the form of more hardened, aggressive, and less educationally ambitious students. The students and the resulting relationships, he insists, are what had kept him there for so long.

For a number of years, Sonny wore both hats: teacher/coach and basketball camp owner. He was unbelievably stretched. Coincidentally, when the teaching started to sour, the basketball camp business started to sweeten. He had always enjoyed the business end but, up to that point, he had not listened deeply to the summer camp melodies. The music finally became its loudest when he had to turn away potential campers because he did not have the facilities to accommodate his growing clientele.

Sonny knew he needed to manage the business full time to build the basketball haven he and so many of the youths craved. He listened to the music, retired from teaching, and started running the business full time. He has never looked back.

Starting today, when you hear the music, turn it up. Do some research. Collect some data. Discover what's playing and why it's playing. Listen for the times the music comes on and for the times it goes off. Think about where you are when you hear it. Think about how it makes you feel when you do. And don't just listen to one type of music; expand your horizon. If it's a triumphant feeling, then keep doing what you're doing. If it's a melancholy feeling, undoubtedly, it may be time for a change. But you're going to have to do something. Awesome people listen to the music and use it to their advantage. Watch them. They are always moving to the beat.

Moving from Average to Awesome

This chapter is not only about wisdom. It's also about how you can effectively deal with, and prepare for, change. This exercise will help you move from an average mindset to a more positive and powerful awesome way of living.

First, consider which statement describes how you think about producing incredible results in the midst of transformation:

- **Average:** You ignore the signals that alert you that it's time for a change or you make excuses for the signals, attributing them to something else.
- **Awesome:** You listen to the music and develop an action plan to produce sensational results. And you're disciplined and diligent while you're making changes.

Second, take some time and consider the questions below. Respond to the questions and be sure to explain your answers. Finally, rate yourself on your progress. If you are currently average, say so (A). If you feel you deserve an awesome rating, indicate that as well (AW). If you are neither average nor awesome but working toward being awesome, just write W.

Getting to Awesome

Key questions	Your response and explanation	Rating
What causes you to ignore the signals when change is needed?		
Do you freeze up when you realize that you have to make a significant decision?		
When going through change, when are you at your best?		

Rate your progress: average (A), awesome (AW), or working toward awesome (W).

Chapter 20

Don't Put Your Goals on Layaway

> The excitement about business and life is the reviewing, the renewing, and the redoing. Doing the same thing repeatedly is only marking time. I desire to make a mark—an undeniable mark—and leave something behind to be fondly remembered.
>
> —RON MITCHELL, PHILADELPHIA

When was the last time you wanted something so desperately you could taste it? That coat, dress, suit, pair of shoes, high definition TV set, stereo, car, cruise, or ticket had your name written all over it. You could smell it, hear it, feel it, and see it, and you would do anything imaginable to get it. You probably visited it in the store window, maybe even took some friends to see it to get their opinion. Whatever hurdles or sacrifices you were going to have to go through—getting up early, going to bed late, saving, working overtime, or creative money management—you were going to do what you felt you had to do. Your life, in your opinion, would not be complete without it. You were on a mission. You were hungry, at least for a minute. Let me explain.

I've witnessed this phenomenon time and time again. I've seen well-intentioned people, not deterred by anything else going on in their lives, getting a short-lived adrenaline rush because of the importance they give a particular event, item, or occasion. I've watched relentless Christmas and Easter patrons shop until they dropped before the big day. I've seen people—after long, grueling, challenging workdays—come home and thoroughly clean their house, then cook all night preparing for huge family Thanksgiving dinners. I've seen sports and concert fans spend the night outside, sleeping on the ground, bundled up in blankets in freezing winter temperatures just to purchase tickets to an event. Somehow, some way, we consistently make time, muster the strength, and put in the effort for *events*—but not for our *dreams*.

But what's more sustaining, events or dreams? If you said dreams, then we're on the same page. To pursue your dreams, you need a special appetite. You have to be *hungreee*!

Colonel Sanders, Mr. KFC himself, was *hungreee* when he wanted to get his tasty chicken recipe on the market. Stories report that at the age of 60-something, he traveled around the world, living in his car, pitching his now-famous chicken recipe. Before receiving his first contract, he supposedly had knocked on over 1,000 doors.

Even Abraham Lincoln endured numerous setbacks. Research suggests that Honest Abe, in several losing elections, received less support than a Vanilla Ice, Fat Boys, and Milli Vanilli reunion tour. Multitudes of successful people paid their dues many times over before finally arriving on the world's center stage. Perseverance became their breakfast, dedication their lunch, and resiliency their dinner and dessert. They were *hungreee*.

Being *hungreee*, on the surface, seems like it could be one of the world's easiest assignments: Identify something you want and steadfastly pursue it with tenacity and vigor. It's this tenacity and vigor, however, that separate the *snacker* from the *hungreee* person. Being *hungreee* requires a phenomenal amount of discipline, drive, determination, self-esteem, and confidence. The hunger required to reach the perceived unreachable or obtain the so-called unobtainable is not sold on shelves or on infomercials. You can't borrow it from a friend or order it online. It comes from within you. And, trust me when I say, "It's not easy!"

Discipline and hunger require doing something you should do when at times you don't want to. You see it in the most dedicated boxers—the contenders—who move away from their families, sentence their bodies to years of grueling, sweaty gym wars and marathon morning runs, preparing for those championship matches. You see it in teachers. They spend their lives earning a modest income, sometimes in disadvantaged surroundings, trying to help us shape our lives. You see it in social activists and protestors. In the name of justice and equality, they risk it all for causes they deem significant. They've faced firehoses, arrests, police dogs, taunts, and guns while demonstrating for voting rights, education, bus-riding privileges, employment, and other human causes.

Consider This: "Some succeed because they are destined to, but most because they are determined to."
—Author unknown

My hunger pangs started early. I started with sports, then eventually landed on more significant tasks like helping people fulfill their dreams and reach their potential.

AWESOME ADVICE

One of my favorite quotes is Emma Goldman's: "If I can't dance, I don't want to be part of your revolution." I love the spirit of joy amidst struggle that it captures. It has energy that lifts me up.

As an educator and activist, I draw on the courageous spirit of those who risked so much for human rights and social justice. I think of Nelson Mandela, Sojourner Truth, Frederick Douglass, Martin Luther King Jr., Anne Braden, Cesar Chávez, Lillian Smith, Harriet Tubman, Gandhi, Malcolm X, and all the other heroes and heroines around the globe who worked for peace, despite the dangers they faced.

Their spirit of resistance and their love for all humanity carries me on the days when I feel like change will never come. They never gave up, and we owe it to them to continue the struggle in any way we can. Helping to create a world of love, peace, and equity for all people (where we can all be free to dance to whatever music we choose) is the most awesome thing I can think of!

—Patti DeRosa, Randolph, MA

While we were growing up, my friends and I woke up *hungreee* and went to bed *hungreee*. We would shovel the snow off of the schoolyard court to play basketball during the winter months. Sometimes we played basketball in the rain. If we didn't have a real football, we used a tennis ball or rolled up pieces of aluminum foil to play two-hand touch. Sometimes we played tackle football in the snow. Our catcher and strike zone was sometimes a chalked-drawn square on the schoolyard brick wall. Sometimes we played baseball at night under the dim, flickering corner streetlights. Our relay races were around-the-block sprints; the two teams simultaneously circled the block in opposite directions as the pavement, street, parked cars, stores, and houses served as our track, field, and stadium. We also learned about hunger from the neighborhood bully, who always sought a rematch if any of us was fortunate enough to get the best of him in a fight.

My hunger was also evidenced in my pushing myself to uncanny limits. I would try to eclipse my personal best time each time I shoveled the snow and raked the leaves. I occasionally rode my bike with my eyes closed and without holding onto the handlebars. I wanted to see how far and how long I could ride without crashing. I used to see how long I could hold my breath under water when I went swimming. I would pinch my nose shut, close my eyes, and then sink to the bottom of the pool. After about 90 seconds I would lunge forward, frantically searching for air. That thrust to get air is the hunger that's needed when you're pursuing your dreams. That was how I lived then and how I now live.

Many of us fake hunger. The pangs are there, but our behavior is not in alignment with our thoughts. We say that we want something badly enough, but our actions masquerade as moments, not momentum. Think about it: In life we don't get what we want, we get what we are. That's why when life starts weeding out the pretenders from the contenders, so many of us succumb. Just to

AWESOME
ADVICE

I believe that life has a turning point—a point at which we either grasp our opportunity to experience awesome or we let it slip away. My opportunity came on the morning of December 19, 1990, at a meeting of the American Society for Industrial Security, or ASIS. As a young, single man and unconnected middle manager in the security industry, I attended that local meeting looking to build my professional network and, in turn, my career. A respected leader in the group asked for volunteers to help him write and produce a monthly newsletter.

I felt like a kid in high school as I looked around the room and watched 50 or so more experienced members stare at their breakfast plates, the floor, their fingernails; they looked at everything rather than make eye contact with the meeting leader. Suddenly I received a kick from under the table from a friend, urging me to raise my hand and volunteer. To this day, I can't understand why he didn't raise his hand instead, but I thank him for his hesitation.

Several months as a writer for the newsletter led to two years as the editor, then to a year each as vice president and president of the local chapter. I was asked to expand my role as a volunteer leader regionally and then internationally as a member of the ASIS Board of Directors. In 2002, I had the honor of being installed as the president of ASIS in my home city of Philadelphia—in front of my family, friends, and 18,000 of the ASIS's 32,000 members.

There's no denying that these accomplishments alone would make anyone feel awesome. But to me, each step has brought treasures and memories to a life that has far overshadowed the titles that I've held. I've made lifelong friends and I met my wife, Lori.

To me, awesome has no laurels to rest upon. It is an ongoing state, achieved by continuously seeking out new challenges—living each day with a purpose!

—Dan Kropp, Collegeville, PA

see how serious and hungry you are, life will humble you. Pain and self-doubt will stare at you in the mirror each morning.

My Titan Susie Fields says she's unstoppable in her actions to support her family's and friends' goals. "To me no means it's on. If someone tells me no, I find another way. I keep on keeping on. I know it sounds corny, but half of success is just getting up off your rear end one more time and trying again. How many times can you quit when success is right around the corner?"

You have to be *hungreee* if you want to restore relationships, too. If I hadn't been on the "I'm mad at my Dad" diet for so long, I believe our relationship could have been saved before he passed away. Many will say they're hungry, that they want to make peace, but they wait around for the other person to initiate things. Life is not a board game. It's not about spinning the needle or rolling the dice. It's something you cannot take for granted.

Because the great majority of us are visual learners, let me give you a few more pictures of what situational hunger looks like. The challenge is making it typical, not-just-in-the-moment, behavior. Create these pictures in your mind's eye. Have you ever seen someone running through the airport to make his or her flight? That person is situationally *hungreee*! Have you ever seen a football player relentlessly running downfield to make a tackle? He's situationally *hungreee*! Have you ever seen shoppers lined up to enter a popular department store that's having a huge going-out-of-business sale? They're situationally *hungreee*! Have you seen the reality show contestants (*Fear Factor*, *The Apprentice*, *Survivor*, and the rest) going for the money and prizes? They're situationally *hungreee*! (I think some of you may believe they're insane.) I'm sure you've seen the movie depiction of two lovers running into each other's arms after a long separation. They're situationally *hungreee*! Imagine if people consistently went after their dreams this way.

This is how we need to pursue our goals, our relationships, and our passions if we want to awesomely fulfill them. Anything short of being *hungreee* is pretending.

Once you are totally committed to this new, improved way of eating—I mean living—consider this seven-step process for *hungreee* management:

Step 1: *Be creative.*

Step 2: *Be intentional.*

Step 3: *Be focused.*

Step 4: *Be courageous.*

Step 5: *Be tenacious.*

Step 6: *Be consistent.*

Step 7: *Be resilient.*

Moving from Average to Awesome

This chapter is not only about drive. It's also about how to discern whether you're serious about a particular pursuit or just going through the motions. This exercise will help you move from an average mindset to a more positive and powerful awesome way of living.

First, consider which statement describes how you think about willpower and fortitude:

- **Average:** You inconsistently go after your dreams and goals. You settle for and complain about your current reality.

- **Awesome:** You're developing an insatiable, unrelenting drive to reach your goals and fulfill your passions. You're developing a *hungreee* attitude for winning, laughing, dreaming, loving, and growing.

Second, take some time and consider the questions below. Respond to the questions and be sure to explain your answers. Finally, rate yourself on your progress. If you are currently average, say so (A). If you feel you deserve an awesome rating, indicate that as well (AW). If you are neither average nor awesome but working toward being awesome, just write W.

Getting to Awesome

Key questions	Your response and explanation	Rating
What situations do you find yourself giving up?		
What situations do you find yourself giving extra?		
Do you have a sustainability or backup approach to help make your drive last longer?		

Rate your progress: average (A), awesome (AW), or working toward awesome (W).

Chapter 21

Reexamine How You See the World and Yourself

> My perspective has changed from being an unwilling receptor of change (a victim) to being a positive participant with the power to make decisions, especially about my attitude, and to contribute where my skills are needed. I've learned that I can bring light or darkness into every situation.
>
> —BONNIE STRAND, BLOOMINGTON, MN

I remember my first day as a Widener University freshman. Deciding what to wear took the better part of my morning rush hour. Because I was now a college student, I wanted to look like one. As I rode the 309 bus to the beautiful, Chester, PA, campus, I reminisced about my high school years and pondered my upcoming college years. My immediate past had been spectacular, but my immediate future was a plot waiting to unfold.

My slate was now clean. Only the Widener football coaches and a few faculty members in the financial aid and registration offices had any idea of who James Smith was. To the remainder of the nearly all-white faculty and student body, I was another spry freshman taking summer classes to help better prepare for the college curriculum. C. Alan Rowe, Widener's legendary basketball coach, was my math professor. I was new, and I was uncharacteristically nervous.

With my self-esteem suddenly deciding to wait for me outside the building, I walked into the classroom. Upon entering, I peered around and was overwhelmed with an unexpected urge to make a speedy U-turn and head back home. "Do I belong here?" I thought. The room was filled with spirited, attractive, confident, 1590-on-their-SATs-looking coeds. Their colorful book bags appeared new. I was still carrying the same worn, over-the-shoulder bag I had carried during my last two years of high school. Even their pencils seemed to have sharper points. They had calculators. I had a ruler and a pencil sharpener.

I reached down, picked up my envious, nervous, demotivated spirit, and carried it to the back of the room. I sat down. My only words during the entire two-hour period were "I'm here," in response to hearing my name during the attendance roll call. This was certainly not like me. I always sat in the front of every room with the other overachievers. I always walked with my head up and with a wide, assured smile and an extra sense of urgency. You always felt my presence. Not this time, however. I let my smudged glasses get the best of me.

Smudged glasses?

Sometimes we wear our eyeglasses for days without cleaning the lenses. For some unknown reason, we don't immediately notice the spots, streaks, or fingerprints. We move through life as if we see the world perfectly clearly. Then one day we have a stroke of genius—an epiphany. Something moves us to find a Kleenex, paper towel, napkin, scarf, shirt, or tie to clean our lenses and voilà! The world becomes a brighter place. Ironically, up to that point, we would have vehemently argued that we could see everything just fine. But what are we missing?

Let's examine this for a moment.

Some of the dirt taking temporary residence on our lenses comes from the atmosphere: rain, smog, pollution, dust particles, and the like. The other smudges are "our stuff," our fingerprints. Just as the literal smudges on eyeglasses affect how we see things, the figurative smudges on our "glasses of life" affect how we move through this world, how we live our lives, how we see ourselves, how we perceive and respond to challenges and opportunities. Or as Alfred Lord Tennyson once said, "I am a part of all that I have met."

The "stuff" we have no control over (that is, Mother Nature and Uncle Universe) is parallel to the people, unforeseen circumstances, and the like we encounter. The "stuff" we do have control over are our emotions, reactions, perceptions, behaviors, attitudes, and thoughts. Many will go to their graves arguing that they see things exactly the way they are. But that's comparable to walking around with dirty glasses.

When our glasses are dirty, very seldom do our friends, relatives, and colleagues come up to us and say, "Hey, your glasses are filthy. You need to clean them." We eventually come to that realization on our own. I had no idea how dirty my glasses were when I stepped onto Widener's gorgeous campus that day. My lenses were filled with smudges of doubt, anxiety, and ambivalence, mostly attributable to my minority freshman student status.

Sometimes when we take off our glasses, our blind spots remain. On those occasions, we should consider being open to feedback and hearing other points of view. I wrote about this in the introduction to this book when I shared that some of my realities and perceptions may stretch some of your beliefs and perspectives.

Consider This: "You can't depend on your eyes if your imagination is out of focus." —Author unknown

---

How else can dirty glasses have an impact on us?

The former *Primetime* television show with Diane Sawyer and Chris Wallace had over the years featured episodes in which professional testers were placed in everyday America. Whether they were trying to find employment or housing, get a tee time, buy automobiles and other merchandise, get into their locked car, catch a taxi, or teach a class of first graders, the inconsistent treatment the testers received based on their age, appearance, gender, physical ability, and race was startling. Even more amazing were the comments of those who provided the inconsistent treatment. To a person, despite the mountain of video evidence and footage that showed otherwise, they said that they treated all the testers the same and that their behavior and decisions were fair. Many, however, declined to be interviewed.

Dirty glasses help shape attitudes, biases, beliefs, and a litany of "isms" and provide many of the high, moving hurdles one has to clear to become awesome. Dirty glasses create self-limiting beliefs and low self-esteem. Dirty glasses can end relationships. Dirty glasses can cause people to always play the blame game, never taking responsibility for their "stuff." Dirty glasses can be detrimental to your health and well-being. Dirty glasses cause insecurity.

Dirty glasses can deflate our "dream" balloons. Consider the decisions we make about employment, family, education, fitness, nutrition, and relationships. Are those decisions grounded in truth

AWESOME
ADVICE

In just seven months I would step down as manager of the Philips Lighting Application Center. As I sat reviewing the latest set of very positive workshop evaluations, I thought to myself, "How close did I come to pushing this opportunity away?" Self-employed or virtually so for most of my professional life, I had been working as a successful project manager on lighting projects in Upstate New York. I was good at it and had more work than I needed. I was content, even happy. I had four grown children, a few grandchildren with more on the way. Life was good.

One phone call would change all of that.

The day was December 28, 1998, three months before my 50th birthday. The phone rang: "Hello, yes this is he (I listened, then laughed aloud). Who put you up to this? Is this some sort of joke?" I asked. The voice on the other end replied, "No, not at all. I represent Philips Lighting Company and we want you to consider being the next manager of the Lighting Center." "Oh yes," I replied, "and what will they put in the announcement, 'Philips hires *plodder* from Buffalo?' The last person to hold that position had a PhD."

Four months to the day later, I sat in my new office in Somerset, NJ, in the Lighting Center, as the new manager of Lighting Education. At age 50, I was "stepping out" when most of my peers were "stepping back."

I came to Philips to do lighting education; it seemed like a good fit. Instead, what I found surprised me beyond all telling; I found my "right" work. As a consultant I was good, maybe even very good. What I had was an average expression for my gifts and talents. As I "unpacked" my role as Lighting Application Center manager, I discovered my gifts and talents as a trainer.

I never would have uncovered these roles as a project manager in Upstate New York. The awesome part is finding my right work and having the freedom to spend the rest of my life pursuing it with a passion!

—Paul F. Hafner, Somerset, NJ

and facts? Have we collected all the data? Have we taken full responsibility and accountability? Have we thoroughly researched all our options? Or do we need to wipe off our lenses?

How many times do we talk ourselves out of opportunities? How many times do we look in the mirror and say, "Self, don't worry about it, it wasn't meant to be. You really didn't miss anything. They weren't going to give it to you anyway. They don't even like you."

One of the reasons I love what I do professionally is that I view motivational speaking, coaching, training, and consulting as jobs in the glass-cleaning business.

My good friend Savannah had worked in corporate America for nearly 30 years. Having worked for two major companies during that time, she had accumulated a wealth of knowledge, expertise, and positive professional relationships. She managed departments and excelled in individual contributor roles. She was respected by her peers and other professional colleagues, and thus was a mainstay in her organizations.

However, her deep-seated drive to start her own company sang in her subconscious like a popular television commercial jingle. The jingle never went away. Neither would the smudges on her glasses that said, "Stay here. It's safe. Why give up all of these benefits. You could never make it on your own. Why start all over again? Most people who go out on their own never make it."

After a few more years on the job and a few more lengthy conversations with her biggest antagonist and her biggest protagonist (herself), Savannah cleaned her glasses of the fear and self-doubt. She took the plunge, leaving her safe, high-salaried *Fortune* 100 job and started her own company. Our last phone conversation lasted less than 30 seconds. She was too busy with client requests and projects. She had to call me back later.

I wonder what was on the lenses of:

- The players of the United States 1980 gold-medal-winning Olympic hockey team before they beat the invincible Russian team in the semifinal game
- Rosa Parks when she refused to give up her seat on the bus
- Marian Wright Edelman when she became the first black woman admitted to the Mississippi Bar and founded the Children's Defense Fund and Stand for Children
- John F. Kennedy when he envisioned us walking on the moon
- David Ho when he was one of a small group of scientists who recognized AIDS as an infectious disease and set out to discover a cure
- Jonas Salk when he developed the Salk vaccine for polio
- Jane Elliott when she first facilitated her "brown eyes / blue eyes" exercise in 1968 on her third graders in Riceville, IA, to teach them a lesson in discrimination
- Muhammad Ali when he had to choose between going to prison and fighting in the Vietnam War
- Lance Armstrong before he mounted his bike for the first time after recovering from cancer
- Jose Rizal when he, through the use of his powerful pen, rallied Filipinos to believe in themselves
- Helen Keller while she spent the most of her life advocating for poor people, women's rights, pacifism, and the rights of people with disabilities
- Steveland Morris (Stevie Wonder), when as a youngster he decided that he wanted to make sensational music by singing and playing the harmonica and piano.

Take off your glasses right now! Take a look at the lenses. How clean are they? What areas need additional cleaning? What areas get smudged the most? What are your blind spots? It's time for a major breakthrough! It's time for you to reinvent yourself! It's time for you to see more clearly! Awesome people have awesome vision!

Moving from Average to Awesome

This chapter is not only about vision. It's also about how to improve your imagination and eliminate self-perceived barriers. This exercise will help you move from an average mindset to a more positive and powerful awesome way of living.

First, consider which statement describes how you think about your life, both professional and personal, and how you view the world in general:

- **Average:** You think you see the world perfectly clearly—that your perceptions and thoughts are unequivocally right.
- **Awesome:** You're reexamining how you see the world and how you see yourself. You're reinventing yourself. You're looking for feedback and information that challenges your critical assumptions and beliefs.

Second, take some time and consider the questions below. Respond to the questions and be sure to explain your answers. Finally, rate yourself on your progress. If you are currently average, say so (A). If you feel you deserve an awesome rating, indicate that as well (AW). If you are neither average nor awesome but working toward being awesome, just write W.

Getting to Awesome

Key questions	Your response and explanation	Rating
Do you ever refuse to change your perception of something despite evidence that proves your view is inaccurate?		
How have you developed your perceptions of yourself and of the world?		
What perception changes do you think are still in order to help you move to awesome?		

Rate your progress: average (A), awesome (AW), or working toward awesome (W).

Chapter 22

Eliminate the Aspects of Your Life That Keep You from Being Awesome

It's not the load that breaks you down—it's the way you carry it.

—LENA HORNE

I woke up at 6:15 a.m. with my office on my mind. The kind of work I was about to dive into was not the usual, however. No reading files. No checking voicemail. No computer work. With energy in my step and creativity in my head, I was on a Feng Shui mission.

I started by throwing out the old magazines. Outdated issues of *PC*, *Forbes*, and *New Jersey* bit the dust first. Next went the old shoes, shoe polish, sneakers, and everything else on my closet floor. All those items were getting a one-way ticket to Goodwill. My ancient, typewritten company manuals and facilitator's guides, which I had not referenced in what seemed like 300 years, were next. I privately escorted them to my garage.

The old file folders also received their walking papers. "Old this," "forgotten that," and "haven't used this in a long time" were all moved out of my home office.

I lit several candles. I opened the curtains. The sun said, "Whassuuupppp?!?!?!?" I rearranged pictures and other important files and could now actually see the plush gray carpet that I've walked on nearly every day for the past seven years but never really appreciated. I cleared my desk—wow, the calendar was actually still there. No, I was not auditioning for an appearance on a fix-up-your-house cable TV show, nor was I participating in some kind of cleaning marathon. My mission: to continue unloading the junk (figurative and literal) from my trunk.

The day before my office rampage, I spent the afternoon receiving coaching and book-publishing direction from my Titan, colleague, and friend Leslie Shields. Leslie and her sister Cydney wrote the book *Work Sister Work* in 1993. Upon entering Leslie's home, I immediately found myself in a mental place of relaxation, serenity, and calm. Every piece of furniture rested in the perfect spot. Imaginary "children under 21 not allowed" signs hung from the walls. Not only could you eat off the floor, you could probably also eat off the welcome mat and backyard lawn.

The living room, where the meeting took place, was *awesome*! The rich, cobalt blue walls, which were not blocked by a bevy of art and other pictures, were empowering and energizing. A Snickers-bar-brown wall unit filled with African American dolls and figurines captured my attention every time my mind drifted from the meeting. Finishing touches included a bronze love seat, cream sofa, brown bureau with computer and printer hidden inside and loving family photos on top, television, stereo unit, and a selection of CDs that reminded me why I'm still in love with the music of the '70s and '80s.

Throw in the sweet fragrance from the candles and the sunlight that attended the meeting, and you had tranquillity, a room that whispered to guests to take off your shoes and chill out. This room commandeered all your stresses, anxieties, and worries.

When I asked Leslie about the room, she said it was her sanctuary, another indication for how she lives her life. "I keep it simple, Jim," she said. "I don't crowd my life or my personal surroundings with too much stuff. It can become overwhelming. Too much to fix, too much to think about, too much to clean. I just keep things basic and simple. My family members are always asking me when I'm going to put paintings on the wall. I ask them why should I cover up these beautiful blue walls? Serenity and simplicity work best for me."

I drove home that evening listening to a CD of Jermaine Jackson's greatest hits and thinking about the incredibly inspiring meeting we had just completed. I spent time prioritizing the 29 items that Leslie and I created for my *From Average to Awesome* to-do list. I also thought about the energy and calm that I felt while in Leslie's home.

My immediate plans were simple: work toward making my office, my surroundings, my work, and my life simpler. Get the junk out of my trunk. There were too many old magazines, manuals, and files in my office taking up the space and room that new books and resources could occupy. All the unused materials selfishly created a workspace of clutter, not creativity.

Junk is anything that prevents you from being awesome. Your trunk is your life.

Literally and figuratively, there are unnecessary things, things we seldom use, that we drive around with for years. These items, from time to time, roll around in the trunk, making enough noise to remind us they're still there. The junk is weighty enough to slow our drive as we head up steep hills. In addition, the junk takes up much-needed space. Given these facts, one would reason that we'd want to remove all the junk from our trunk—and fast.

Instead, we take it with us everywhere, moving other items around to make room for it, eventually storing new "stuff" in the back seat. You need proof? The next time you leave the grocery store after an hour of food shopping, and you pull your shopping cart full of groceries up to your trunk for loading, you'll know what I'm talking about.

Metaphorically, the junk in one's life trunk can be like kryptonite. Kryptonite? Remember the powerful superhero Superman? Despite the bulging muscles that stretched his tight, blue superhero uniform to the bursting point, Superman had a weakness: kryptonite! He did his utmost to avoid this green substance that rendered him helpless and powerless. And if not for Lex Luther and the other villains who indefatigably attempted to curtail the man of steel's crime-fighting career, Superman would never have come into contact with it.

The difference between Superman and us was that the man with the muscles avoided kryptonite, his junk. We hold on to ours for dear life. We work for ours. We cellphone ours every day. We page ours. We date ours. We check in with ours about important life decisions. We spend Saturday afternoons polishing and buffing ours. We log onto ours. We eat and drink ours and buy more when we run out. We look for kryptonite qualities in the people we date. Sometimes we ask others if we could borrow some of their kryptonite. Some of us never leave home without it. Kryptonite is deadly junk! It kills our drive and our spirit. We have to get it out of our trunk.

Bronwen, a close friend, recently told me about how her friend Denny summoned the courage to get rid of his kryptonite. She related how his sales job was causing him severe pain. As a result, he was going through life rather than growing through life every

AWESOME
ADVICE

My Feng Shui consultant and career coach put the keys in the trunk and turned. The trunk popped open and staring at me was years of junk—and a business relationship that was killing me.

For about eight years I had been selling a pregnancy product to insurance companies and women's health centers. During the later part of this time, a struggle developed between the product's publisher and me. In major denial, I viewed the struggle as just a bump in the road—telling myself that things would eventually improve when sales and other business initiatives righted themselves. I just had to keep my focus on the vision.

But our struggle continued. Our view of what needed to happen for the product continued to differ. Our relationship was really strained. Things began to get funky financially, too. My growth within the company came to a standstill. My focus on the vision became fuzzy, but I kept plodding along. I believed that we had worked together too long to bring things to an end.

Then Tamra came into my life. She immediately realized that something was causing a great deal of pain and sapping my energy. She asked me, "When will you be done with this relationship?" I said, "In three months' time," even though up until she had asked the question I didn't even know an end was in sight. Coincidentally, during this same time, the publisher said that she would be going in a new direction and that she believed our business arrangement should come to an end. I agreed wholeheartedly. Rather than trying to convince the publisher that I should be a part of the new direction, I simply let go. And when I did, I allowed space for something more spectacular to come into my life. If it weren't for Tamra, I probably would have fought to keep my old, stressful arrangement. I needed help and I got it.

—Bettina Carey, Seattle

day. On the surface, the job seemed OK, but it was toxic. It was killing him! Kryptonite, 100; Denny, 2.

People saw Denny as a hard-working, corporate professional. He made good money and had super benefits. He definitely needed these bennies; he was married with two young children. Relatively speaking, on the outside he appeared to be very successful. But on the inside, his spirit was eroding. The inner conflict (he hated what he was doing, he wasn't being creative, and the job was crushingly routine) was taking its toll. Have you ever had a job that you disliked so much you dreaded driving anywhere near it on your days off? That was Denny.

Sleepless nights, mood shifts, and inertia were as common to him as jewelry is to QVC and Mr. T. One day he came home, sat down at the kitchen table, and began to cry—one of those heaving, sniffling, heartbreaking, can't-catch-your-breath sobs. His wife Judy took a front-row seat. Trying to compose himself, Denny said, "I'm spiritually and emotionally dead. I hate my job." "Well, what do you want to do?" Judy asked. "I want to create beautiful furniture and art objects for people, to create a beautiful home for someone," he replied. Judy, to her credit, did not go rapid-fire into the myriad family responsibilities and obligations they shared. She simply said, "Well, then, that's what we're going to do."

Shortly after his kryptonite meltdown, Denny quit his job and started his own business. Those were some lean years, he had told Bronwen: "Sometimes we couldn't put a meal together and we had to accept help from Judy's parents from time to time; that really bothered me." Gradually, Denny's clients began to spread the word about the generous, warm man who designed incredibly beautiful furniture and art objects. As his confidence grew, his apparent love for his work became an uplifting statement to those who met him.

Soon, Denny advertised in the *Wall Street Journal*. He has since done work for Bill Cosby, Carolyn Roehm, the Smithsonian

Institution, and former secretary of state George Schultz. Not only does he create beautiful objects for his clients, but he also imparts his effusive joy for living. He got rid of the kryptonite that was in his trunk.

Consider This: "Life without hope is a life without meaning." —Author unknown

Let's keep it real. Kryptonite and other junk are not going to go away merely because you say, "Kryptonite, junk, it's time for you to get your hat and coat and leave." This stuff is powerful. If you don't get rid of your kryptonite, it will get rid of you!

Junk can also take the shape of a longtime friend whom you allow to soak up too much of your precious time with the same draining, depressing sob stories. Every time you see him or her you cringe, thinking about enduring the upcoming soliloquy. He or she may even become irritated because you appear happy, and ask "Why are you so happy?"

The junk in your trunk can also be the television set that you turn on as soon as you wake up in the morning or when you return home after work or that you watch well into the night and early morning.

Junk can be the barrels of "other people's stuff" that you carry with you each day. You go to work thinking about their problems. You think about their problems during the workday. And you think about their problems as you drive home from work. That's what you call going to work before you get to work, working, then working overtime as you go home. We get so absorbed in everyone else's front lawn that we find little time to pull out our own weeds.

What's more, we overuse the proverbial excuse, "Well, he needs me. He would do it for me." It's just that you never give him an opportunity to help you because you're always helping him. Certainly, there's nothing wrong with lending a helping hand or ear. Some people, however, attempt to use their "help credit card" when they know the available balance is in the negative.

Once you begin your unloading, you certainly could benefit by having an awesome supporting cast (like Judy, Denny's wife). The first step, though, is to assertively declare that you're going to rid yourself of that power-draining source, and then do it! Other tools for this arduous job include prayer, commitment, discipline, stick-to-itiveness, courage, and desire. If your junk is a person, you will have to change the script and rewrite the role that person plays in your life. If your junk is an object, ask yourself, until you're blue in the face, does my junk move me closer to or further away from the person I want to be?

You're going to need a new routine and a new reward system, because there's retention in repetition. And you're probably, unfortunately, going to have to experience an enormous amount of pain. I've come to realize that many of us don't make changes until it *really, really* hurts.

If we are going to go on this journey from average to awesome, we have to ask ourselves how we can make our travels swift and less cumbersome if we're carrying around junk. And when we do have to scale that steep hill called drama, the junk will undoubtedly keep us there a lot longer than if our trunks were empty.

An additional point to consider: Sometimes the junk in our car is so quiet we forget that it's there. Remember, kryptonite radiates. Just bring your car—your life—to a sudden, immediate, abrupt stop and your kryptonite will roll to the front. What a reminder!

So, are you ready for awesome? The next chapter will give you additional breakthrough tips for your journey. But please do not begin reading the next chapter until you've started to remove the junk from your trunk. You would not want anything to slow you down now, would you? Here's a cheat sheet for getting the junk out of your trunk: discard it, unload it, rewrite the role it plays in your life, avoid it, and forget its phone number. Remember, you are not powerful when you are around it. Just remember Superman.

Moving from Average to Awesome

This chapter is not only about simplifying your life. It's also about how you have to rid yourself of toxic people, toxic employment, and toxic habits. This exercise will help you move from an average mindset to a more positive and powerful awesome way of living.

First, consider which statement describes how you think about your personal stumbling blocks:

- **Average:** You move through life carrying the weight of other people's problems and your life's hiccups into every day.
- **Awesome:** You're proactively addressing the aspects of your life that make you sluggish—those things that slow you from being your awesome self. You're eliminating the bad habits, time drainers, and toxic people that make noise in your life, like junk in your trunk.

Second, take some time and consider the questions below. Respond to the questions and be sure to explain your answers. Finally, rate yourself on your progress. If you are currently average, say so (A). If you feel you deserve an awesome rating, indicate that as well (AW). If you are neither average nor awesome but working toward being awesome, just write W.

Getting to Awesome

Key questions	Your response and explanation	Rating
What are some of the bad habits you have to get rid of?		
How are you currently managing your kryptonite?		
What type of support do you need to help you with this transition?		

Rate your progress: average (A), awesome (AW), or working toward awesome (W).

Chapter 23

Enjoy Today as Another Adventure in Your Awesome Journey!

> As a firm believer in the "oneness" of humankind and the fact that we're all on many individual journeys, I selfishly recognize that making the world better for others is in fact making the world better for myself, as well as paving a smoother path for my next journey.
>
> —BARRY CALLENDER, NASHVILLE

I'm not average, and neither are you. I want to be happy, and so do you. I desire the best for everyone that I come to know, and this book is one giant thank-you card. I thank you for the cheers and for the jeers, but most important, I thank you for the many lessons recounted here—your gifts to me.

I really got to know myself during the initial writing, then revising of *From Average to Awesome*. Replaying the memories and experiences that shaped who I am was both painful and centering. Talking with others in the midst of their awesome journey was also both trying and revealing. And attempting to craft a book that shared my hurdles and hurrahs on the road to extraordinary living in a way that didn't make me come across as trite, commercial, pompous, or angry was probably the most challenging task.

Writing this book might have been easier if I had disappeared from the workplace or had gone into seclusion. I could have taken an extended vacation somewhere in the mountains and just written. I could have stopped taking calls and shut down my business operations for some time. But I made the conscious decision to live my life and run my business as usual, but with just a lot more late-night and early-morning typing, both in hotels and at home. I chose this path because I did not want to put my journey to awesomeness on pause and because I wanted to continue to collect insights, anecdotes, and lessons for the book.

Consider This: "No matter what your lot in life, build something on it."
—Author unknown

I mentioned in the book's introduction that my goal was to share anecdotally and through my Titans, colleagues, and friends how I've moved from average to awesome. To make this happen, I said I would share a number of hurdles I've had to clear to get there. One of those hurdles, and perhaps the most difficult to discuss, was race. Actually, during my first few drafts, I barely mentioned race. I felt that was the safe way out—it wouldn't cause anyone to close the book in disgust—but it did not totally reflect my story.

Through this dilemma, I learned *not to censor my spirit, my words, and my thoughts.*

After reading an early draft of my manuscript, Patti DeRosa, my friend and diversity mentor, told me to stop talking in code. She said to be clear, concise, and to say exactly what I meant. I knew, after that feedback, that I had to write to express, not to impress. I had to write to disclose, and not to babysit other's reactions to my realities.

I couldn't leave it up to the reader to read between the lines to uncover my truths. As I revisited the text, I began to wonder how often I had talked in code during my corporate days.

I then sensed that some of the experiences I would share would surprise some of my colleagues and upset others. In the eyes of my peers and colleagues, I've always been hard-working, driven, committed, and amiable Jim Smith Jr. Many of my white friends had never heard me discuss issues of race and how I thought the unfair treatment I received at times was more than just corporate politics and miscalculated judgment. Nor did I ever share that playing Jackie Robinson got tiresome sometimes, and that I missed not seeing and working with more black corporate leaders and professionals. I toiled in corporate America for a number of years, and during that time I grew and matured into the person I am today. Yes, race was *one* of my major hurdles to awesomeness, but there *were others*, many others. I was challenged with sharing this message without sounding like "the angry black man." Helping people to appreciate and understand their plight (for example, class, education, family, gender, parenting, race, and education) is a daunting task, especially when theirs is so different. Nevertheless, it's my story and I'm sticking to it.

For any journey, you need to take fuel along.

My fuel was my beliefs, together with my family and friends who supported me during my moody, unproductive, idea-less, fatigued moments, and my numerous colleagues who helped with editing, ideas, encouragement, and support. As I continue on this awesome journey, I will never forget to pack their pictures and words in my suitcase and in my heart. Waking up in the middle of the night in some hotel room, in some city, will never be the same. I will awaken to pictures of my Titans on my nightstand.

Frank Sinatra sang, "Regrets, I've had a few, but then again too few to mention." I guess that about sums up my professional journey—and maybe yours, too. I worked for three industry leaders and learned plenty about myself professionally and personally. I also learned that I can be awesome no matter what! And that's what I want you to take with you. Say goodbye forever to excuses. Know that "but" is an argument for our limitations and that when we argue for our limitations we get to keep them. You have to get out of your own way and hold yourself responsible for your tomorrows.

Being awesome is a choice. It's about transcending barriers and being true to oneself at the same time. It's living with passion and with a purpose. It's not cursing the establishment. It's getting the establishment to see your greatness. When it comes to being awesome, good enough is not even close to being good enough. Step up! Bring it! Fire hard, kid!

I hope this book has challenged you to go searching. Hey, really, I'm no one special. I'm Jim Smith Jr., Gina's husband, Nanci's oldest son, Rodney's brother, and Daecia, Ian, Lauren, and Jordan's Dad. I don't possess any superpowers, and I didn't graduate from college in two months. I'm just like you. I've worked extremely hard; you've read about my blood, sweat, and tears. I can't recall too many things that were just handed to me. I had to go after them. And this effort has become part of who I am. If there's no test, then there's no testimony. If there's no mess, then there's no message. That's why I know anyone can be awesome. But you have to be open to pain and possibilities, and push back and be persistent. When in trouble, I go back to my roots, my lessons, my beliefs, and my Titans.

The consulting firms I've partnered with have also added to my "awesome stew." One group in particular helped me solidify the certainty in my mind that I wanted to take my professional training and speaking to a larger audience. I was one of their groupies for eight years, chasing this supreme training and consulting group from training conference to training conference, inhaling their plethora of creative training techniques, until I finally received my uniform in 1998.

During my journey, I've also learned to "shake it off" and stay focused and *hungreee*. I've winced and then have come back. Benjamin Mays said, "It must be borne in mind that the tragedy of life does not lie in not reaching your goal—it lies in having no goal to reach." And when others demonstrated through word or deed that they were not on my team, I used their taunts like a pole vaulter uses his or her pole to clear the bar. As Les Brown says, "Don't get even, get ahead. . . . Let personal and professional happiness be your panacea."

One day, when I met my photographer Pat Harmon at Barnes & Noble, I had no inclination that we were going to put the ribbon around this book writing project before I left. I was there to discuss our upcoming photo shoot.

After two hours of photo talk, we moved into an update on my book. Excitedly, I explained that I was nearly finished, except for a powerful closing. Pat stood up and said, "Follow me." We walked over to the section where the other motivational and inspirational authors lived—Gotham Chopra and Iyanla Vanzant, James Redfield, Kristine Carlson and Erin Brockovich, Les Carter and Katie Couric, Gary Zukav and Richard Carlson, Pat Croce and Jim Smith Jr. Yes, Jim Smith Jr.! I saw *From Average to Awesome* on the Barnes & Noble shelf! I felt a rush of exhilaration! I knew that some day soon I would return and buy a copy right from this very shelf.

With my Jim Brickman CD playing in the background, I began to bring the first edition of this book to a close. My journey to awesomeness is ongoing. I still have a little junk in my trunk

AWESOME ADVICE

I am a dreamer, a true romantic. I always have been and I always will be. I count on me. No one else can bring me down. I have become an awesome person simply by dealing with each new step on my life's journey, no matter how painful or how embarrassing. I have learned from every boulder that landed in front of me. I have learned from both the things I fell victim to—and those things that were out of my control—and also by the poor decisions I've made. I believe that some of the most beautiful, honest, and loving people are those who have truly *lived* and have truly *learned*. I have! Life's journey is just that: a path given to us to walk and learn from each step of the way. It isn't meant to be straight; we'd never learn that way.

—Nancy Rebecca, Chicago

to remove and some baggage to discard. My glasses need to be cleaned every now and then, and I have to monitor my "you can do anything" zeal at times. I have to be mindful not to take on bad business. And I will spend more time with my Titans and continue to make my life simpler and achieve more balance.

I know that there is plenty still to learn. Although I'm on an endless pursuit of awesomeness, I'm still going to bump my head. I'm still going to fumble the ball every now and then, and I'm not always going to make the best decision. I've learned that the journey is more important than the final stop.

We pick up passengers and experiences, memories and mentors, trials and testimonials. But one thing I will do is keep exploring, keep asking questions, and keep pushing myself. Isn't that what the journey is all about? I'm *hungreee* for knowledge. I'll continue to call on the lessons I've shared with you as well as those that I'm sure are coming my way.

I have not done my best work yet! I'm still moving from average to awesome! How about you?

Moving from Average to Awesome

This chapter is not only about your giving and receiving. It's also about how you can incorporate your life lessons and experiences into your todays and tomorrows. This exercise will help you move from an average mindset to a more positive and powerful awesome way of living.

First, consider which statement describes how you think about your journey to awesome:

- **Average:** You take life as it comes, from one day to the next. You're reactive rather than proactive.
- **Awesome:** You realize that every day is another day in your journey. You're making every attempt you can to make the next

day better than the one before. You're learning from the insights you obtain along the way and making a difference.

Second, take some time and consider the questions below. Respond to the questions and be sure to explain your answers. Finally, rate yourself on your progress. If you are currently average, say so (A). If you feel you deserve an awesome rating, indicate that as well (AW). If you are neither average nor awesome but working toward being awesome, just write W.

Getting to Awesome

Key questions	Your response and explanation	Rating
Do you talk about your journey with others?		
Do you appreciate both the good and the trying legs of your journey?		
If you had the opportunity to change something, what would you do differently?		

Rate your progress: average (A), awesome (AW), or working toward awesome (W).

Chapter 24

Take Ownership of All That Happens—It's All an Awesome Challenge

My grandmother Fannie Mae Gillis, who I rarely saw as I was growing up, had a profound effect on me. Regardless of where she was, you felt her power. Everybody in my family called her Momma. She was very spiritual, intuitive, and positive. I remember one particular life-changing moment we had when I was a little girl. Having noticed that I was not happy, she came up to me as I was lying in bed and said, "Gina, regardless of what happens, everything is going to be all right, baby; everything is going to be all right." She said it twice. Nothing else. Her words penetrated me. I have held onto those words my entire life. No matter what trials, tribulations, valleys, or heartaches I've encountered, I've known that everything was going to be all right.

—GINA M. SMITH, MOUNT LAUREL, NJ

People clapped. They cried. They roared with giddy laughter. They cheered, "Go Jim. Go Jim. Go Jim. Get busy. Get busy. Get busy."

Afterward, they stood in a looooooooong line to buy and have me autograph their copy of the first edition of *From Average to Awesome*. This felt incredible. I was beaming. "I could really get used to this," I thought to myself. It had all finally come together. I did it! This two-year writing project, which took me back through my childhood and all the way up to my present, was a taxing, painful, but needed journey. There had been many memories, many warts, many tears, and many lessons. But as Gloria Gaynor sang, "I Will Survive." And I did.

My Titans, family members, colleagues, and others turned out in significant numbers. The tiny theater on Broad Street in Philadelphia, typically used for jazz shows, was bursting at the seams with over 200 people for the launch of my book. This was July 30, 2002. The book, *From Average to Awesome: 41 Plus Gifts in 41 Plus Years*, officially took its first step and I was well on my way to huge things. . . . Or so I thought.

I had dreamed of some semblance of a book tour, with book signings and additional speaking opportunities after that night. In that dream, I'd envisioned feature stories in the local Philadelphia newspapers and national magazines as well as in *USA Today*. I also hoped that a major publisher would come in and sign me to a book deal. Oprah? Of course, I was going to be on her show and in her book club.

Things didn't pan out that way, however. Instead of admirers, opportunities, and success, the things that stood in line waiting to enter my life were challenges, problems, misfortune, and humility. In the long run, they turned out to be more gifts and lessons, but they sure didn't feel that way at the time.

Yes, articles were written about me. Both Temple and Widener, my two colleges, kick-started things. A couple of the smaller local newspapers wrote features, too. My overtures to other magazines and newspapers didn't quite work out.

Securing a literary agent was also a "swing-and-a-miss" proposition. That's not uncommon for self-published authors, but it still didn't sit well with me. "Just meet me and read my story, you'll want to take me on as a client," I believed. This was wishful thinking.

Consider This: "Perhaps the best thing about the future is that it comes one day at a time." —Author unknown

Actually, there were some book signings. These became powerful lessons in humility, though. My brother and I set up a number of them, mostly in Philadelphia and Delaware. After the first several signings, it dawned on me that few people knew who I was. I had spent much of my adult life in corporate America, and no one had heard of Jim Smith Jr. I hadn't embezzled or laundered money from my organizations. I hadn't changed my identity. I didn't have a surreal story. I hadn't starred in a Tyler Perry movie. I wasn't an Olympic gold medallist. I hadn't overcome a debilitating sickness. I hadn't pulled a family from a burning house. I hadn't sold 3,000 books from my car trunk yet. And I didn't yet have a recognizable name in the African American community, unlike Charles Barkley, Colin Powell, and Johnnie Cochran, each of whom had a book published around the time the first version of *From Average to Awesome* initially came out. "Also unlike those guys," I thought in frustration, "I wrote my entire book all by myself; I didn't have a ghost writer or a cowriter." But readers generally want to read about someone they've heard about. My story, in the public's estimation, wasn't yet ready for prime time.

I remember those first signings as though they happened yesterday. I would sit either inside or outside the bookstore at the book-signing table (with my books placed neatly and strategically by my side) watching people look at me, trying to figure out if I was somebody. My smile and encouraging wave didn't work too often. I sat there thinking that there *will* come a time in my life when these bookstores were going to be packed. Folks would be dying—I mean living—to meet me and buy my book. The ironic thing is that I would be (in my mind) the same person then as I was now. But they would view me differently. That was my motivation, my drive. Until then, at least at that point, it was another mall, another bookstore, another 2 to 10 books sold. Thank goodness for my motivational speaking gigs and clients. That's when I sold hundreds of books. People got the opportunity to see me do my thing. . . . And in front of their very eyes, I became somebody.

The next challenge: My second marriage was falling apart. It took its toll on me. Everyone knows how trying separation and divorce can be; I don't have to belabor that point. In addition, my little pumpkin, my daughter Daecia, and I had to reinvent our relationship. Seeing her only every other weekend, and sometimes during the week when I drove from Philadelphia (I initially moved back in with my mother) to New Jersey to take her to school in the morning, was very different. I often cried when we had to say goodbye.

I remember when I knew for sure that things were not going to work out in my marriage. I drove to Daecia's school, pulled her out of class for a few minutes, and gave her nonstop hugs and kisses in the hallway. She said, "Daddy, you're silly." I told her that I loved her tremendously. She went back into the classroom, and I went back to trying to organize my life, which was becoming increasingly humbling. I was a 41-year-old author, international speaker, consultant, and professional trainer now living with my Mom. Wow—that's certainly not where I had planned to be at this point.

It got better—I mean worse. Business slowed up immensely. Opportunities were harder to find than a New Year's Eve party without resolutions, alcohol, or dancing. I went into January 2003 with just one workshop on the calendar. In February, there were two. Creditors began calling with a vengeance, and my clients, when I did secure some work, didn't send in their checks quickly enough to help me manage my mounting debt. "I've been here before," I thought. "Why now? Why me? I just finished my book! Where's the reward for all my hard work? This 'awesome' thing isn't easy!"

My other awesome discovery was what I learned about me. No matter what the world sends my way, I do my best to live an awesome life every day. Nevertheless, I was growing tired, frustrated, and impatient with people who didn't seem to be trying as hard as I was, especially if I had to interact with them. Because of my business and travel activities, I was running into plenty of them. Airline security personnel, cab drivers, waiters, hotel staff, and other customer service providers were becoming daily challenges. (Of course, not all these professionals fell into this category, but I encountered enough to last several lifetimes.) They seemed generally unhappy about what they were doing or whom they were doing it for, and it showed in the service they provided. They were grouchy, curt, disrespectful, and argumentative.

I would become annoyed because I let their behavior bother me (rather than ignore it), and I was disappointed that they weren't doing something about it. I developed a bad habit of wanting to help people fix their situation when I sensed their displeasure. I was consistently losing sight of the notion that people will change when they, and only they, choose to change. I was also forgetting the fact that some people must perform jobs they didn't choose just to survive—to keep a roof over their heads and food on the table—and that I should cut them some slack. I didn't like the impatience and lack of empathy I was discovering in myself; I had to so something and do something quickly.

I reread my book.

I rededicated my life to being awesome.

AWESOME
ADVICE

The greatest gifts I have been given in life are my children, Aaron and Dana. When my husband and I were considering starting a family, I thought it would be as easy as making the decision to have children, getting pregnant, and, nine months later, adding the joy and love of a child to your life.

I came from a big family. My Mom had five children. I just knew that my husband, Chris, and I would be great parents. We decided to start a family right after we were married. Within a few months, I became pregnant. Yes! Everything was working according to plan and falling into place. However, just two months into my pregnancy, my glee was dashed by a miscarriage. This was an extremely difficult time, but everyone assured me that this was just a bump in the road to parenthood. We were told not let this dim the light of our "family" dream.

Getting pregnant a second time took what seemed like forever, but we were committed. I finally tested positive again. Days flew by as we made it past the three-month mark. We were well on our way to being parents! As my belly began to grow, we planned, decorated, and created a magnificent nursery where I envisioned that we would nurture, love, and care for our baby. I was six months pregnant and beaming. Everything was perfect until that snowy Saturday in November.

Once again, we lost our baby.

This loss was heartbreaking. We knew this baby and felt we'd created a lasting bond. I was devastated.

It wasn't until my third miscarriage that doctors had given me a less than 50 percent chance of ever carrying a child. At first I was crushed. I had accomplished everything else in life that I had put my mind to, but it was beginning to look like I would never have children. In time, I began to accept that realization, convincing myself that it was OK. We decided to adopt, but then I became pregnant again. The doctors were very grim, offering no more than a 20 percent chance of a positive outcome. We were very realistic about the potential risks and outcomes. It was an extremely long 10-month pregnancy. Finally, Aaron, our gorgeous baby boy with curly hair and deep dimples, was born.

There were several more miscarriages along the way, but three years later, my daughter Dana arrived. Our family was complete. It was only through the years that followed that I came to realize that the wonderment and joy of parenting is in living each moment with our family. As we enjoyed those moments, I've had the privilege of influencing and being influenced by my children and their friends. My children are grown now. Both have completed college and are on their own. We continue to share in their ups and downs, and most important in their love. Looking back, I knew there were many times when I thought I would never be able to ever give birth. Moreover, there have been times when I thought I was a terrible parent. My children have taught me that it's not so important that I am an awesome parent but that we are an awesome family. We can continue to endure every challenge and make it together!

—Marilyn Massaro, Weston, FL

I vowed to learn from my postbook experiences, realizing that those experiences have only made me stronger.

I promised myself to always be a leader, to make lemonade out of the lemons that are bound to come my way. I had to work on my mindset. That's where everything starts.

How does one do it? In addition to the other lessons I've mentioned in the previous chapters, consider these seven "next-edition, what-I've-been-reminded-of" tips:

- Shift your mindset to ward off distractions. Sometimes this means not responding to something that you know is wrong or off base, or responding in a way that doesn't prolong the disagreement or conversation. Become mentally impenetrable.

- Become "You, Incorporated" (that is, take care of yourself, invest in yourself, protect yourself, and take pride in yourself).

- Avoid trying to fix everyone's problems, regardless of who he or she is. Remember, people are not always going to do things the way you'd like them to. Their reality is different from your perception of them.

- Expect challenges, especially when you appear to be handling things in a positive way. Be proactive, not reactive.

- Keep showing up for life every day. My theory, as it relates to dealing with the world each day, is: Wake up, get up, show up, step up, then shake them up!

- Own who you are. Stop making excuses (and conjuring up reasons) for your shortcomings. Own your stuff. Confront your demons. Stop blaming others.

- Take good written and mental notes on your conversations. Always get clarity. Miscommunication causes confusion, confrontation, and consternation.

"Awesome" is a way of life. You truly have to understand yourself before you can begin to understand others. This is vital because we let others make an impact on our realities so often. You may want to consider some sort of transformation work to get to the core of what may be preventing you from being awesome. If you really want to change and improve, you have to become a lifelong student.

As for me, I still have a wonderful relationship with my daughter. We do "Daddy-daughter" stuff all the time. From homework and spelling tests over the telephone to taking in movies and visiting bookstores on the weekends, we are continuing to grow, not simply go, through life. Several years ago, we even spent eight wonderful days in Spain. One of the highlights of our trip was flying there and back first class.

Business has picked up tremendously. This book has played a key role in creating many new opportunities. And I have done two other books, *Crash and Learn: 600+ Road-Tested Tips to Keep Audiences Fired Up and Engaged* and *Masters of Success*, coauthored with Ken Blanchard and other powerful speakers. I've continued to surround myself with incredible people. I've remarried—a beautiful, spiritual woman, Gina. We have a blended family—Lauren (23), Jordan (15), Daecia (12), and Ian James (2), our newest arrival.

Most important, I feel more awesome than ever. I welcome challenge, and I welcome change. I still have more work to do—awesome people are always busy!

Moving from Average to Awesome

This chapter is not only about character building. It's also about how life continues to serve up unexpected, humbling challenges. The following exercise will help you move from an average mindset to a more positive and powerful awesome way of living.

First, consider which statement describes how you think about personal ownership, responsibility, and accountability:

- **Average:** You're resting on your laurels, thinking that past accomplishments will carry you for an extended period of time.
- **Awesome:** You're constantly moving forward with self-enrichment and improvement, taking ownership of all that happens to you. You're learning from your highs and your lows and leveraging both for better tomorrows, realizing that things are not always going to go the way you'd like regardless of the work you put in. Also, you're giving others the time and space to grow at their pace, not yours, and in a direction they, not you, have chosen.

Second, take some time and consider the questions below. Respond to the questions and be sure to explain your answers. Finally, rate yourself on your progress. If you are currently average, say so (A). If you feel you deserve an awesome rating, indicate that as well (AW). If you are neither average nor awesome but working toward being awesome, just write W.

Getting to Awesome

Key questions	Your response and explanation	Rating
Do you try to fix everything—for both you and others?		
Do you admit when you're wrong?		
Do you own all your results?		

Rate your progress: average (A), awesome (AW), or working toward awesome (W).

Chapter 25

Do Something Different This Time—Get Out of Your Comfort Zone!

> After I read a powerful book, I immediately share it
> with others. I do that for two reasons. One, I want to
> promote what I read. Two, I want the people who I've
> shared it with to hold me accountable. I then write the
> key takeaways in my special church book. I randomly
> read through it during services. Most important,
> though, I try to come away with the *one* thing, from the
> entire book, that I'm going to do to make a difference.
>
> —TONYA MURPHY, PHILADELPHIA

Just this one last chapter to go. Congratulations! I sense your adrenaline beginning to build. Self-help and personal empowerment books are written to do just that. You're probably thinking about all the changes you're going to make in your life. You've convinced yourself that you're ready for the

AWESOME
ADVICE

If someone were to pick three characteristics to describe me, they would probably say strong, intelligent, and direct. After all, I survived molestation, rape, and abuse and used my story to motivate young women in my community. I advanced through the ranks of corporate America, at one point advising CEOs without even having my college degree. My pace in life forces me to be direct and my time is precious and I don't want to waste it.

Unfortunately, these positive characteristics were only evident when I was in my element—surrounded by family and friends who loved me and at work with peers who admired me. In my comfort zone, it was easy being Uneeka, a force to be reckoned with. But what about outside my element?

After going through a painful divorce that left me a single mother of five children, I was offered a job in Tampa. Accepting this offer would force me to leave all my family and friends and the church I had attended for 16 years. Without my support system, would I be strong enough? What if I failed? What if I succeeded? I wasn't sure of what scared me most, success or failure.

I remember sitting in church one Sunday, and my pastor said, "To get what you never had, you have to do what you have never done." I purposed to make a list of all the things I had never yet had: (1) to love and raise my children the way I want to, (2) to be free from people's expectations of me, (3) to stand on my own feet, (4) to be happy, and (5) to feel successful. I realized that to fulfill these never-yets, I was going to have to step outside my comfort zone.

So, I read a number of books. I began to reach out to the mentors and truth tellers in my life. I shared the possibilities of the move to

Tampa. Some were skeptical. They wanted me to think through the entire process and be confident in the decision I made. I was advised to consider the children. I was reminded that I had just built a house and that I had several job offers on the table. "Why change now?" one person said. "What will we do without you?" said another. My soul was screaming, "Go!" My insecurities were screaming, "Stay!"

I had one last person to call. He was someone whom I considered a mentor and friend. I prayed that he would give me some advice to sort out my feelings. In the middle of my explanation for why I could not accept the job, he interrupted me—"Listen, you are going to be successful in this position. You have people who you can call when you hit a brick wall. I am one of those people now." Jim's reassurance was invaluable. The next call I made was to my pastor, advising him that I had decided to take the position.

Two years later, I live in Tampa and I responsible for the training, quality, retention, and patient satisfaction of a $589 million company. I have learned things that I would never have learned in Ohio. While attending ministry school, I met a wonderful man who broke through all my hurt and pain and captured my heart. We are married and raising our five children. I took a risk and stepped out on faith. The reward I received is the reward of finding me. I know who I am and what I stand for. I know what I like and what I do not like. I realize that I am strong, intelligent, and direct in my element—and beyond! In life, to grow, you sometimes have to be repotted. I feel awesome.

—Uneeka Jay, Tampa

world! Where are Rocky and the Philadelphia Museum of Art steps when you need them?

What's going to make this postreading experience different from your others? The typical postreading routine includes, *but is not limited to*, things like this:

1. You make a new to-do list with at least 50 items.
2. You tell your friends that you're on fire—that you've just read a life-changing book.
3. You loan this book to one of them and never get it back.
4. You buy another copy of this book and never leave home without it.
5. You change your eating and sleeping habits.
6. You join LA Fitness, Bally's, Gold's Gym, or the like; buy new workout gear—gotta' look good while you're getting your workout on—and vow to exercise every day.
7. You treat people more kindly.
8. You buy a journal and begin to record your goals and daily experiences.
9. You consider yoga, meditation, Pilates, or spinning.
10. You stop everything after two weeks, returning to your former way of living.

This book has been about moving from average to awesome. I've offered myriad ideas, and I hope that you've decided on several. No, I didn't serve them up in order. Instead, they were introduced in a more thematic way. Now it's time to look at the very big picture: What does being awesome ultimately mean in your life, and what are you going to do differently this time? How about getting out of your comfort zone?

I've found that most people who don't sustain their pull-through or action plan after reading something inspirational fail for these kinds of reasons:

- They let personal and professional stuff get in the way.
- They get distracted.
- They still have fear and insecurity.
- They feel they have so much to do that they become overwhelmed, and they finally decide they'd rather stay in their comfort zone.

I don't want these kinds of things to happen to you. Here are the excuses to avoid, in no particular order:

- You don't want to be by yourself.
- You have a lot of haters in your life.
- You have a ton of family obligations.
- You're in too much debt.
- You owe taxes.
- You have relationship woes.
- Your blended family isn't blending.
- You're afraid of taking risks.
- You've never tried it any other way.
- You're too busy.
- You work too many hours.
- You've convinced yourself that people don't respond to you the way you want them to.
- You fear the unknown.
- You constantly think, "What if I fail?"
- You don't know of anyone else who's done it.
- You don't have the money.
- You want someone else to go first.
- You watch too much television.
- You don't have any support.
- You have a ton of bad habits to break first.
- You determine that your situation isn't that bad.
- Your family talks you out of it.

- Your family makes life too easy for you.
- You're afraid of conflict.
- You're a behind-the-scenes person.

I don't need to keep going—I'm sure you get the idea. There are many, many really good excuses. But people who move from average to awesome *abhor* excuses. I think that's why my friends never call me to have a pity party.

Consider This: "We make our decisions, and then our decisions turn around and make us."—R. W. Boreham

---

It's time for you to be repotted. It's time for you to grow to be awesome. Consider the previous 24 chapters. Which ones are you going to apply to your situation first? What about the key average-to-awesome questions at the end of each chapter? What questions are you going to address immediately? Promise me that you'll do something different this time. You can start by saying goodbye to comfort-zone thinking. As a reminder, earlier in the book you were encouraged to incorporate these steps:

1. Commit to being awesome.
2. Form a dream team and an advisory board and meet with them regularly.
3. Share your dreams with others.
4. Address your questions with others.
5. Develop an action plan and a contingency plan.
6. Choose from the awesome side of the menu every day.
7. Put your dreams on a clipboard that you look at every day.
8. Always remember the law of attraction (that is, you attract what you expect and what you think about).

9. Keep a journal of your experiences.

10. Pray. Pray. Pray.

I believe in you. It's your time to be awesome! I wish you the very best!

Moving from Average to Awesome

This chapter is not only about doing something different this time. It's also about how you have to commit to *being* the difference—that you hold the keys to your success. This exercise will help you move from an average mindset to a more positive and powerful awesome way of living.

First, consider which statement describes how you think about moving from average to awesome:

- **Average:** You live a life in your comfort zone. You occasionally take risks, but for the most part you follow your daily, monthly, and yearly routine. You situationally talk about making changes, but that's it. Every year is the same for you. But you're not in enough pain to make the life changes that you so desire.

- **Awesome:** You live a life of reinventing yourself. You stare fear down. You frequently put yourself in new, different situations to test your resolve. You have a wonderful support system. When you get knocked down 9 times, you get up 10 times. You're not addicted to television or any other vice. You live each day to the fullest. You help others on their journey to awesomeness, and you believe in yourself.

Second, take some time and consider the questions below. Respond to the questions and be sure to explain your answers. Finally, rate yourself on your progress. If you are currently average, say so (A). If you feel you deserve an awesome rating, indicate that as well (AW). If you are neither average nor awesome but working toward being awesome, just write W.

Getting to Awesome

Key questions	Your response and explanation	Rating
What's going to keep you on track when life starts to fire darts at you?		
What are you going to do next to reinvent yourself?		
What's your greatest takeaway from this book, and how are you going to apply it to your life?		

Rate your progress: average (A), awesome (AW), or working toward awesome (W).

ABOUT THE AUTHOR

According to the many thousands who have participated in his moving motivational keynote presentations and workshops, Jim Smith Jr. is one of the most energetic and passionate speakers and trainers who have come along in recent times. He really connects with his audiences, encouraging them and challenging them to be outstanding. His speaking style evolved, he says, from his ups and downs in corporate America, education, professional and college sports, parenting, and marriage. It's this awesome journey that has taken him from a small second-floor, two-bedroom apartment in West Philadelphia to inspiring and motivating both national and international audiences.

Upon his graduation from college with a degree in English,

after months of receiving form letters of decline, Jim secured his first corporate opportunity. Before putting on the suit and tie every day, however, he set his sights on professional football, a dream he had held for some time. He had realized his other sports dream, winning a national college football championship, during his junior year. He vividly remembers sitting in the stands all teary-eyed when the Philadelphia Stars cut him, and his dream, from the team. He knew, however, that many more of his dreams would come to fruition. And he was right!

He is also author of *Crash and Learn* (ASTD 2006) and coauthor with Ken Blanchard of *Masters of Success* (Insight Publishing 2006).

To find out more about Jim and the services he provides through JIMPACT Enterprises, visit www.jimpact.com.